Core Concepts of Project Management

Core Concepts of Project Management

David L. Olson

 BUSINESS EXPERT PRESS

First published in 2020 by
Business Expert Press, LLC
222 East 46th Street, New York, NY 10017
www.businessexpertpress.com

ISBN-13: 978-1-95152-756-3 (paperback)
ISBN-13: 978-1-95152-757-0 (e-book)

Business Expert Press Portfolio and Project Management Collection

Collection ISSN: 2156-8189 (print)
Collection ISSN: 2156-8200 (electronic)

Cover image licensed by Ingram Image, StockPhotoSecrets.com
Cover and interior design by S4Carlisle Publishing Services Private Ltd., Chennai, India

First edition: 2020

10 9 8 7 6 5 4 3 2 1

Printed in the United States of America.

Abstract

This book addresses project management in the context of general project management. An introductory chapter discusses project features in general. Part I of the book focuses on the important human element in project management. Part II discusses two processes involved in the initial project definition stage, as well as covering estimation. Part III involves planning, and also deals with project risk and implementation. A feature of the book is an effort to tie content to that of the Project Management Body of Knowledge (PMBOK). Each chapter includes reference to how each chapter relates to the PMBOK structure and relationship to the 2020 PMP Exam Outline.

Keywords

project management; human factors; project implementation; project organization

Contents

Preface

This book addresses project management in the context of information systems. It deals with general project management principles, with focus on the special characteristics of information systems. It is based on an earlier text,[1] but shortened to focus on essential project management elements.

Key features are a shorter introduction to project management, focus on general project management, updating of Project Management Institute (PMI) material, and serving as an introduction to quantitative material in the companion book.

The first chapter presents various statistics indicating endemic problems in completing information system projects on time, within budget, at designed functionality. While successful completion of projects is a challenge, there are some things that can be done to improve the probability of success. This book reviews a number of project management concepts. These include developing organizational ability to work on projects, discussed in Chapters 2 and 3. Sponsor expectations can be based on better information if a good job of project selection is conducted, as discussed in Chapter 4. Better systems development (to include requirements analysis and project work breakdown structure—Chapter 5) can assure that proper resources are acquired to accomplish a project. In projects with greater time pressure, agile methods are often found appropriate (Chapter 6). Projects involve high levels of risk, and schedule delays are often encountered. Chapter 7 discusses some related methodologies. Chapter 8 will discuss the importance of critical success factors in the context of project implementation.

This first book discusses the people and initial process aspects of project management. Each chapter identifies related PMI material. The companion book will cover important tools available to help successfully manage projects.

Note

1. Olson (2015).

CHAPTER 1

Introduction to Project Management

Key Points
- Characteristics of projects
- Projects as systems
- Basic project—critical success factors

Almost every organization gets involved in many projects. A major reason projects are so important is the fast pace of change and the more specialized nature of modern business. Many of these projects involve information systems, a distinctive type of project. Firms have to keep at least close to the cutting edge for harnessing the power of computers in almost every aspect of business. Large accounting firms have enlarged their information systems consulting operations, and almost all of this type of consulting involves an information systems project. This means that there are more and more unique activities drawing people together from diverse locations and diverse organizations with diverse, specialized skills.

Project management has long been associated with operations management and is an important topic in operations management's curriculum. There has been an explosion of projects in the field of information systems. Information systems project management involves some characteristics that are different from those found in operations management, but many of the same tools can be applied. This is primarily due to the volume of new projects that organizations have adopted to implement computer technology. There are many useful things that information technology can do for organizations. The information technology environment involves high turnover of personnel, turbulent work environments, and rapidly changing technology. This results in high levels of uncertainty with respect to time and cost. Despite this more volatile environment, project management principles applicable to operations management can often be transferred to the information systems environment.

What Is a Project?

A project involves getting a new, complex activity accomplished. Many activities qualify as projects. Building the Golden Gate Bridge, transporting the Statue of Liberty across the Atlantic, and the attempt to elect Barack Obama as president were all major projects. So were the development of the atomic bomb and sending men to the moon.

Each political campaign is a marketing project, just like other marketing projects to sell new products. You have each written a paper, which was assigned as a "project." These projects involved researching some topic and organizing ideas into a cohesive, rational whole. In football, developing a promising young quarterback prospect is often a multiyear project, including intensive coaching to learn the team's offense, to learn the style of teammates, development of leadership skills, passing technique, and building endurance and strength. What television viewers might view as natural talent may have involved the closely planned and coordinated activities of quite a large number of people.

Projects

- Involve a definable purpose
- Cut across organizational lines
- Are unique activities

Projects are purposeful in that they are designed to accomplish something for the organization undertaking them. Projects usually cut across organizational lines, drawing people from a variety of functional specialties. Constructing automobiles on an assembly line is no longer a project once the assembly line is developed, because it becomes a closed, repetitive activity that continues as long as anyone can foresee. Making a series of sales calls is not a project, because it is not a unique activity. However, just like the first assembly line, the first round of sales calls is a project, until a desired level of competence is attained. Projects include:

- Constructing something
  - a road, a dam, a building, an information system
- Organizing something
  - a meeting, an election campaign, a symphony, a movie
- Doing anything the first time
- Accomplishing a new, complex activity

Project Characteristics

Because projects involve new activities, they typically involve high levels of uncertainty and risk. One of the reasons assembly line operations are efficient is that everyone does the same thing over and over, hour after hour, day after day, year after year. This repetitiveness allows high degrees of specialization, which in turn enables greater productivity. The activities of many different people and machines can be balanced for maximum efficiency in an assembly line operation. **Projects involve lower degrees of efficiency** than are obtained in assembly line operations.

Because of this higher degree of uncertainty, it is much more difficult to estimate the level of resources required to accomplish a project than it is for other forms of productive organizations. It is also more difficult to estimate the time required (which amounts to another resource). Many projects are late, but not all projects take longer than estimated. The Russian atomic bomb project was completed ahead of schedule, and about the same time, the U.S. U-2 airplane project was finished in about one-tenth of the estimated time. Yet, projects finished ahead of schedule are still rare. **Projects are collections of activities**. If one activity is late, other activities often have to wait for it to finish. If an activity is ahead of schedule, those doing the work tend to be more careful, or slow down for other reasons. The activities that follow often cannot start early anyway, as the people and materials for those activities may not be available until the originally scheduled starting time. For these and other reasons, it is far more common for projects to be late than to be finished early.

Because of their temporary nature, projects inevitably involve gathering together a diverse group of specialists to accomplish a variety of tasks. Project team members often will not know each other very well, at least in the beginning of the project. They will tend to be quite different people, with different skill sets and interests. The primary feature of a project is that it is a **set of temporary activities conducted by ad hoc organizations.**

Information systems projects have many similarities to generic projects. They consist of activities, each with durations, predecessor relationships, and resource requirements. They involve high levels of uncertainty and often suffer from time and cost overruns, while rarely experiencing time and cost underruns. However, information systems projects are different from generic projects in some aspects. While each project is unique, there are usually many, many replications of the types of information systems projects. Most are served by a standard methodology, with the need to identify user requirements, followed by design of a system, production of the system, testing of the system, training and implementation, and ultimately maintenance of the system. These steps are not always serial, with many loops back to prior stages. They involve the need for specialists in different areas of the information systems field, but these specialties are not as distinctly different as carpentry and electrical work. Systems analysts usually know how to program, and testers know all of the other functions involved in a project. Project team members from the development side usually understand each other well. Information systems projects of course involve computers, which is a distinct characteristic that has more impact than what might have been apparent initially.

Types of Projects

Projects in the engineering world tend to involve a lot of uncertainty (especially with respect to how long they will take). But information systems projects have added levels of uncertainty. To demonstrate these differences, let us consider four types of projects: engineering (construction), political, movies, and information systems.

First, engineering projects involve more physical activities, while the other three types of projects involve people creating something. It can be argued that engineering projects are thus much easier to manage, because scheduling is a matter of calculating physical quantities and using past production rates to determine how long activities should take.

Second, information systems projects require specialists with different skill sets to work together to create a software product. Movies are similar in this respect. There may be a variety of skills needed for political projects, but for the most part, it is public relations—working with the press to put your candidate in the best light and getting maximum positive exposure. (Some specialists may be needed to cover up negative exposures.) Information systems and movies involve lots of different specialties. Movies need actors, a staff to make actors happy, camera people, directors, grips, and lots of other things. Information systems projects need system analysts, programmers and/or software developers, testers, system installers, trainers, and other specialty skills.

Third, projects involving humans creating things are much more difficult to estimate, because it is more difficult to estimate how long a creative activity (like writing a bug-free code) will take. Actually, political campaigns are more predictable because there is an end point—voting day. Effectiveness might be hard to estimate, but duration is pretty much given. Movies also have planned schedules, but directors may feel that artistic creativity was lacking in scheduled shots and insist on redoing them. Information systems clearly involve less certainty as to duration than the other three kinds of projects considered here.

Dimensions of Complexity

Projects can differ on a number of aspects. These include the number of people involved and the diversity of skills involved. Some projects are individual efforts to accomplish something. Others, like a major military campaign, can involve hundreds of thousands of people. The more people that are involved, the greater the need to organize into subunits, requiring a higher proportion of managers and thus a lower proportion of productive people. In general, the more complex the project, the more time and resources required.

Group size dimensions can vary over extremes. A few examples of projects for different sized groups, ranging from individual effort through three general group levels, are given for comparison.

Project Size by Size of Group

Individual:	A term paper is often an individual effort. Making an oil painting of a landscape is an individual project.
Group:	Organizing a wedding can be a major project for a small group. Implementing a computer system may involve a small group project. Each audit is a project conducted by auditing specialists.
Organization:	Construction organizations are created to develop efficient skills at building structures of one type or another. As each project is completed, there is often a great deal of change in personnel, although the organization will retain some of its people for the next project. Information systems consulting organizations follow a similar pattern.
Multiorganization:	The space shuttle involves coordinated activities of many people. Probably the most involved projects known to mankind are also the most wasteful. World War II involved the radical reorganization of entire countries, relocation of entire industries in the Soviet Union, long marches in China, the rebuilding of entire industries in Germany and England, and development of entire new industries in the United States.

Projects can also differ on the dimensions of uncertainty. It is much more difficult to predict how much time is to be required the first time you do something. Since projects are usually things done for the first time, they usually take longer than expected when they were estimated.

Information systems currently are in very high demand, outstripping their supply. Another possible bias is introduced by the practice of making initial estimates intentionally low to get work. This bias improves the probability of getting work, which is often negotiated on a cost-plus basis. This practice is not at all recommended, as it leads to a bad reputation when initial promises are not kept. Furthermore, it has ethical ramifications with respect to truth in advertising. An additional factor in project lateness is that large government projects are the most commonly reported. These projects tend to be very complex and often overrun time and budget. How many times have you read about a government project of significant magnitude taking less time than estimated? Since there is a strong correlation between time and money, late projects almost always cost more than expected. When was the last time you heard of a government project having a cost underrun?

General project management is a field that has developed primarily since World War II. With more complex undertakings, many project management principles have been developed. They typically involve a cost/time/quality trade-off, found in almost any project. Specifically in the information systems field, this trade-off can be stated as follows:

In the field of information systems, there is an old adage that you can have any two of three things in a project. You can get it done on time, you can get it done within budgeted cost, or you can get it done well. If you are willing to wait, you can get the job done right within cost. If you are willing to spend the money, you can get a good job done quickly. Or, you can get the job done on time and within budget, with the only reservation being that it will not perform as specified.

This adage is not presented as a recommended way to treat all projects. We all like to think that we can do better than anyone else and accomplish all three tasks. But over and over, in the fields of construction, government projects, and information systems, problems in completing projects on time, within budget, and meeting specifications have been encountered. Project management cannot be blamed for all of these reported failures. The point is that we should understand the difficulties involved in a project environment, seeking to understand the project as a system so that we keep it on target with respect to accomplishing what it is intended to do, in the most timely and efficient manner possible. Bringing in a project on time, within budget, and meeting specifications is tough. Project managers need to expect difficult challenges.

Modern Business

Business has grown much more complex, with interrelated currencies and stock markets. The pace of business is at the speed of light, as stock trading is conducted electronically, oftentimes by artificial intelligence systems. Information technology markets are less predictable. The outputs of many companies are tied together through just-in-time systems with dedicated suppliers. At the output end of production, producers and retailers are often connected through electronic data interchange. The international aspect of business is typified by arrangements such as GATT, NAFTA, and the European Economic Community. The rapid pace of change has resulted in the disappearance of many companies, age-old organizations like the Southwest Conference, and entire countries like the Soviet Union.

In the rapidly changing world of business today, there is a growing need to manage projects intelligently. Project management advanced a great deal in the defense, aerospace, and construction industries. Techniques developed for controlling the interrelated activities of many different organizations and crews can be applied to the field of information systems, which includes many projects to install new applications or to tie old applications together.

Project Management Systems

Projects are systems. Subsystems found in project management systems include a technical core, a control subsystem, and a project information subsystem. The **technical core** includes the technical expertise and equipment that gives the system the ability to accomplish what it needs to do. Expertise can include systems analysis, program development, testing, installation, and user training skills. Equipment in a broad sense can include software, such as CASE tools and subroutines, that improve productivity.

The **control subsystem** is the means management has to control operations. Within an organization, this control subsystem coordinates the technical core with the outside environment. In an institution, an example of a control subsystem is the board of directors, which approves goals and strategies for the organization (which are usually generated by top management). In a project management system, control includes procedures specified for specific tasks, milestones to mark the completion of project phases, and the expertise available within the project team to solve problems when they are encountered. The **project information subsystem** gives management measures of how the system is accomplishing its objectives. Project information systems need to record the current status of activities, list responsibilities, planned and actual durations of activities, and cost expenditures.

The value of viewing projects as systems is that the total view of the project in light of its intended purpose is clearer. Projects consist of many interrelated tasks, done by different people with different skills. If each task was accomplished in isolation, many suboptimalities would occur. Possibly specific tasks would be done faster or at less expense if the rest of the project was disregarded, but the focus of each member of the project team should be to accomplish project objectives and not to optimize production of specific tasks. If trade-offs exist between task accomplishment and project accomplishment, the systems view makes it clear that overall project considerations come first.

Systems provide a useful framework within which to view projects. To make projects work, project managers need to be able to anticipate the consequences of planned actions. They need to develop an organization system, through hiring and training appropriate, qualified people, within budget. They need to be able to know who they have to deal with outside of the system, for supplies, materials, regulation compliance, etc. They need to understand how to measure how the project is progressing and what controls are available if the project does not progress as planned. Understanding the concept of systems makes it much easier to see the impact of the principles of project management.

Project Entities

A number of people are needed to make projects work. We have stated that user involvement is important. One reason is that they are the client (**stakeholders**). The client paying for or controlling the project is the **sponsor** (sometimes appearing in the form of a project board), causing the project to be undertaken. Related to the sponsor is the **project champion** (sometimes another synonym for sponsor). A project champion may not have authority, but has influence at the budgetary authorization level, and often serves as a cheerleader in keeping top management support for the project high.

The **project manager** coordinates the efforts of people coming from a variety of functional areas. Project managers also need to integrate planning and control costs, by assigning tasks and schedules to the members of the project team.

The **project team** is a group of people with the required skills to accomplish the project. They will often come from different places with radically different skills and backgrounds. Oftentimes these project team members will enter the project (and leave) at different times, making for an even greater degree of turbulence. People who work on projects need to be very flexible and to learn to work with various people.

The **project management system** is the organizational structure used by the project manager to get things done. The project management system includes the information system to provide project team members with the necessary information, as coordination between groups is critical to integrate activities. Organizational structure involves procedures to ensure accurate communication and completeness of activities.

The Project Environment

Successful implementation has been found to require mastery of the technical aspects of systems along with an understanding of key organizational and behavioral dynamics. There has been a great deal of study of information systems **project failure**. Failure can arise due to failing to meet design objectives. Projects also can fail with respect to time and budget constraints. Seemingly successful projects may fail because their intended users do not use them. And finally, systems may not meet the expectations of stakeholders.

Most information systems projects have been reported to be much less successful, reflecting in part a very turbulent environment where many changes are needed. Quite often, management gives up and changes direction. This is not always possible to do.

Numerous studies have been conducted on factors that lead to the success of a project. These factors include planning, user involvement, good communication, and sound monitoring of projects. Additional factors that are repeatedly reported as important for the success of information systems project include top management support and a clear statement of project objectives.

Three factors have consistently appeared as success factors in project failure. These factors, which are also found in general kinds of projects, comprise the following:

Client involvement
Top management support
Clear statement of project objectives

Summary

Project management has many features that are different from those of repetitive operations. These include:

- Lower degrees of efficiency
- Operating in a much less predictable market with more rapidly changing technology
- The need to coordinate more parties and organizations
- A highly dynamic environment involving temporary tasks

Projects are systems consisting of interrelated parts working together to accomplish project objectives. There are a number of important roles within information systems projects. Project managers have to balance technical understanding with the ability to motivate diverse groups of people (the project team) brought together on a temporary basis. Managing this team requires organizing in a way that groups can coordinate their diverse activities. Project champions play an important role in obtaining organizational commitment to projects.

While there are many valuable information systems projects that have been completed, the development environment is very difficult. Rarely do information systems projects get completed on time, stay within budget, and fulfill specifications simultaneously. Top management support to projects has repeatedly been found to be critical to information systems project success. User groups need to be consulted to find out just what systems will be required to do. Systems designers need to be involved to make sure that new systems fit in with the overall organizational information system. Programmers need to be involved to ensure realistic production rates. End-users need to be involved to ensure the quality of systems by making sure that they are usable and useful. After planning, many meetings need to be held to coordinate the project through acceptance and completion.

This book is based on an earlier text, now in two parts. The first book covers project basics. The second book focuses on the quantitative tools of project management. This chapter has presented various statistics indicating endemic problems in completing information systems projects on time, within budget, and at designed functionality. While the successful completion of a project is a challenge, there are some things that can be done to improve the probability of a project's success. The book reviews a number of project management concepts. These include developing organizational ability to work on projects, as discussed in Chapters 2 and 3. Sponsor expectations can be based on better information if a good job of project selection is conducted, as discussed in Chapter 4. Systems analysis and design is covered in Chapter 5 and agile forms in Chapter 6. Chapter 7 discusses the impact of risk and the means to assess responsibility for schedule delay. Chapter 8 discusses the importance of critical success factors in the context of project implementation.

Glossary

Control subsystem. Means to manage project operations.

Project champion. Cheerleader who keeps motivation for the project going.

Project entities. Types of people involved in the project.

Project failure. Standards for project goals that are not met (budget, time, quality, as well as stakeholder expectations).

Project information subsystem. Means to monitor accomplishment of project objectives.

Project management system. Technical core, control subsystem, and project information system.

Project manager. Coordinator of the project, responsible for project success.

Project team. Staff undertaking the project.

Sponsor. Client paying for the project.

Stakeholders. Clients—those for whom the project is being undertaken.

Technical core. Expertise and equipment providing the means to accomplish the project.

PMBOK Items Relating to Chapter 1

A project is a temporary endeavor undertaken to create a unique product, service, or result.

Project management is the application of knowledge, skills, tools, and techniques to project activities to meet project requirements.

A stakeholder is an individual, group, or organization who may affect or be affected by a decision, an activity, or an outcome of a project.

Stakeholders include all members of the project team as well as all interested entities that are internal or external to the organization.

13.1 Identify Stakeholders—process of identifying the people, groups, or organizations that could impact or be impacted by a decision, activity, or outcome of the project; analyzing and documenting relevant information regarding their interests, involvement, interdependencies, influence, and potential impact on project success.

13.2 Plan Stakeholder Management—process of developing appropriate management strategies to effectively engage stakeholders throughout the project life cycle, based on the analysis of their needs, interests, and potential impact on project success.

13.3 Manage Stakeholder Engagement—process of communicating and working with stakeholders to meet their needs/expectations, address issues as they occur, and foster appropriate stakeholder engagement in project activities throughout the project life cycle.

13.4 Monitor Stakeholder Engagement—process of monitoring overall project stakeholder relationships and adjusting strategies and plans for engaging stakeholders.

Thought Questions

1. What makes something a project as opposed to the alternatives?
2. Find and compare sources seeking to identify project-critical success factors.

PART I

The Human Element

CHAPTER 2

Human Factors in Project Management

Key Points
- The role and definition of the job of a project manager
- The importance of communication in projects
- The importance of establishing and maintaining project scope

---

A great deal of the effort involved in making a computer software project work is to get the project development team to work together. This is often difficult, because many computer software developers view life much like engineers and scientists. Their emphasis focuses on getting computers to work. Computers have no feelings, and do exactly what they are told. This environment leads to those people sometimes using a rather abrupt and curt mode of communication. Their ability to communicate effectively with humans is occasionally curtailed. Effective management of teams of software developers requires understanding both their personal tendencies and those of users, usually a quite different personality type.

Information systems projects involve the need to coordinate the efforts of a diverse group of people. One of the most difficult (but also one of the most lucrative) jobs in the world right now is information systems project management. These people have very high-pressure jobs, with a lot of demands upon them, and they tend to have a lot of turnover. However, project managers with experience are paid very well.

Information Systems Project Features

Information systems projects promise a great deal of benefit to organizations. There are many kinds of information systems projects. Enterprise resource planning (ERP) systems are very large scale, possibly central-izing all information systems support for an organization. ERP systems can be built in-house, but usually are purchased software systems. Instal-lation of an ERP is a very large project, often involving interorganiza-tional elements (including vendor and consultant personnel), but little systems development and programming. Web systems are at the other extreme. They are a very useful means of implementing e-commerce and e-business (and other e-whatever), but usually are small scale, and can be turned over to one specialist who does everything. (There may be good reasons to have a team specialize on developing many websites, and there is a definite need to work with users.) Conventional information systems projects often consist of a series of development activities, referred to as a **waterfall model** (see Table 2.1) because if all goes well, results of prior stages spill down to the next stage. (In reality, a great deal of looping back is encountered.)

Table 2.1 Waterfall model of software development with systems personnel

Stage	Personnel
System feasibility analysis	**Systems analysts**, users, finance
Software plans and requirements	**Systems analysts**, users
Product design	**Systems analysts**
Detailed design	**Systems analysts**
Coding	**Programmers, testing**
Integration	**Systems analysts, programmers, testers, systems administrators**
Implementation	**Systems administrators, testers**, users
Operations and maintenance	**Maintenance**

Source: Information systems personnel titles in bold.

Systems analysts have the job of identifying what the needs of the system are, and then designing an appropriate software product. This in-volves the need to understand business problems and to talk to business users, as well as the ability to understand the technical domain and to talk to computer personnel. **Programmers** are usually specialists who talk to computers, and make them function. They can do a more complete job if they talk to humans as well, but some specialize. Testers are very important personnel who try their best to find flaws in systems. Sometimes testers obtain character traits reflecting this critical attitude, but to do their job well, they need to be very meticulous. Systems administrators have the job of implementing software on server systems. This tends to be even more computer-centric than programming. Maintenance personnel are responsible for fixing bugs that are encountered, as well as keeping systems up to date with hardware and software system changes.

There are other information systems job titles as well. For instance, there are workers in database management, in providing help to users, in linking networks together, and many other specialties. Some of these may well be involved in specific projects. But generically, Table 2.1 lists the primary information system specialists found in conventional information systems projects.

Working in this environment, regardless of job title, is very interesting and can be very rewarding. However, it can also be very frustrating. There is a need to not only be technically competent, but also to be able to work with a variety of types of people. There is a need to work with users, who have problems that computer systems hopefully will solve. There is also a need to work with technical people, from systems administrators through coders and testers.

Individual characteristics are the result of different personalities, of individuals with different demographic backgrounds as well as education and experience. These different people find themselves in different organizational roles, with different status levels. Individuals also have different psychological make-up, in the form of needs, interests, and goals. Within information systems project teams, a specific type of personality tends to predominate, focused on technical matters. But members of these project teams need to work with users, who tend to have psychological characteristics more common to the general public, focused on dealing with people, with a broader organizational focus.

Being part of a **project team** can lead to conflict. The degree of conflict is expected to depend upon team size, heterogeneity, and leadership. The larger the team, the more likely for some conflicts to arise, although it can be possible for antagonists to avoid each other in larger teams. The more diverse the team, the more likely conflicts are to arise. Within information systems teams, there tends to be a common technical focus, except for those whose specialty is training. However, sometimes having too many shared interests can lead to conflict, as there can be different opinions about how to proceed technically, and individuals may feel that other people are not competent, whereas in actuality they may simply have a different technical approach. Team processes can play a role in conflict, through the ability to communicate efficiently, and through the relative degree of participation encouraged. Team history may well play a major role in conflict. Working together in the past is usually viewed as a positive factor in conflict, but can be the worst case if personalities clashed in previous project efforts.

Characteristics of projects can also lead to greater levels of conflict. A major factor is time pressure. Some people thrive under pressure, others react adversely. Projects often involve pressures. They also often involve constraints, in that the ideal level of resources may not be available. Some people find that unacceptable, and refuse to proceed with project efforts. Others cope somehow. The more flexible approach is usually more productive. Other factors include success criteria (expectations) and top management support. Without top support, projects tend to be starved for resources, making the work environment difficult.

Organizational characteristics can also be important. Matrix organizations (to be discussed in Chapter 3) involve a very hectic kind of environment, highly suitable for information systems projects. However, it may not be suitable for specific individuals. In matrix organizations, there is a need for actors to quickly adapt to new circumstances, and to deal with new people, new responsibilities, and in general, be able to prosper in a highly dynamic environment. If this is not the type of working climate desired by a specific individual, that individual should find one of the many other professional fields to work in.

Interpersonal conflict can manifest itself in at least four levels. **Interdependence** is the process of people working together, realizing that their success depends on the cooperation of others. This is the form of team unity most desirable in an information systems project team. There will always be disagreements that arise. This is healthy, and reflects thought and effort applied by team members. (If there were no disagreements, this is an indication that some of the team members do not care.) The process of interpersonal conflict becomes disruptive if interference results, from disagreements escalating into actions taken to force one position at the expense of another. A higher level of conflict arises when negative emotions arise, as in heated arguments.

There are a number of different management styles available for team leaders to cope with interpersonal conflict. These styles include problem solving, compromising, asserting, accommodating, and avoiding. The appropriate style depends upon circumstances. Only by understanding human behavior can team leaders learn which style is needed. This selection can be an important factor in project success, system success, individual performance, and effective organizational performance.

Conflict and Performance

Conflict management is essential in obtaining positive information systems project outcomes. Conflict can be useful, in generating better solutions, but harmful behavior is counterproductive in any environment. The bottom line of this result is that it is better to avoid interpersonal conflict in the first place rather than rely upon project leadership ability to mitigate it. Features that might improve information systems project success include:

1. **Project scope and objectives communicated to all of the project team**

   Management often feels that once a project is officially adopted, everyone should automatically rally behind it. They therefore omit a detailed explanation of what the project is designed to do for the organization. This often leads to some resistance to the project by those who were not consulted in the decision, especially those who feel that their input would have been important.

   A related issue is the scope of the project. If the project scope is not clear to everyone, those who make decisions related to the project will not be in a position to make the best decisions. Additionally, user requirements need to have assurance that they are feasible. This is easier to assess if clearly stated acceptance criteria are present. Every requirement should include a definition of what makes system performance acceptable.

2. **Business rationale for undertaking a project disseminated**

The business reasons for adopting an information systems project usually are not disseminated. This is often the case because there are no sound business reasons for adopting such projects, especially those in time-constrained environments. (In Chapter 3 we will argue that business cases are very difficult, because they require estimation of impact that is nearly impossible accurately.)

3. **Accurate project budgets**

In rushed projects, budgets may not even be created. Even if they are, it is very common for such budgets to overlook, or grossly underestimate, some key factors. Budgets, however, are important tools for project control.

4. **Project support present**

Rushed projects never have unqualified support. Some organizational members may continue to oppose such a project long after its adoption by top management. This opposition can manifest itself through open opposition, or simply by small means of uncooperative behavior to delay the project or to reduce its likelihood of succeeding.

5. **Project control firmly established**

Within organizations, there are always issues concerning control. Good project team unity is the best way to deal with such issues. In rush projects, personnel should be selected considering their ability to work under pressure. In information systems projects involving vendors, related issues often arise. Vendors have their own agenda, with the client organization's welfare rarely taking top priority. Control of vendors (and consultants) is key to project success where vendors (or consultants) are present.

6. **Rules not changed during project execution**

A common feature of project environments, involving specialists assigned on short-term bases, is vanishing resources. Vanishing resources refers to assigned personnel who are often unavailable, especially during key periods. Project manager efforts to complain to the permanent managers of such resources often lead to hostility and greater lack of cooperation. Timely and accurate feedback throughout the project is a way to overcome this potential problem.

Political aspects of information systems projects can be very important for project success. This is complicated by the fact that there will always be those who feel that their own interests are furthered by project failure. Human aspects of information systems projects are very complex, and tax the ability of project participants to get along with other people, and to gain progress individually as well as for the benefit of the organization.

Another obvious key need in making a project work is communication. Without clear and accurate communication, project members cannot be expected to know what they are to do, and whom to contact for information.

Project Managers

It has been reported that over 30 percent of new software projects are canceled before completion, and that over half are more than 180 percent are over budget. A commonly cited reason is poor project planning and management. At the same time, there is a shortage of qualified, large-scale project managers.

Project management involves getting work done through outsiders. We will see in Chapter 3 that projects often involve dual lines of authority. Project managers are not in as powerful a position as managers in other forms of organization, and therefore they have to rely on influence and persuasion to get people to work toward project ends. The survival of a project manager depends a great deal on the strength of the alliances that the manager can make with powerful stakeholders and the success in competing for resources within the firm. The project manager's mission is to integrate diverse activities in a highly dynamic environment, to produce technical deliverables with a team whose members are temporarily assigned from different parts of the firm and therefore have other loyalties. This must be done within the constraints of a budget for cost and for time, and meeting quality specifications.

The project manager has to make decisions and provide a sense of direction for the project's organization, and serve as the hub for project communication. The ability to take on a number of roles is required. The project manager must be an evangelist, to keep everyone believing that the project will work. He or she must also be an entrepreneur, getting the necessary funds, facilities, and people required for project success. The project manager must also be a change agent, orchestrating diverse activities and facilitating these efforts to ensure project success.

The project manager has the responsibility of all managers, to get the job done on time, within budget, and satisfying specifications. The job also includes planning and organizing, dealing with groups representing the owner, and subcontractors. In addition to people skills, the project manager must understand enough technology to realize what is possible and what is not, and to recommend project termination if things are not working out. The project manager needs to be personable, to use a leadership style capable of motivating diverse people who do not work directly for the project manager. The project manager also needs to be able to understand budgeting.

Comparison: Functional and Project Managers

Project managers have to operate in a very turbulent environment. Table 2.2 shows that there are many differences between the jobs of a project manager and a functional organization manager.

Table 2.2 Comparison of managerial features

Functional manager	Project manager
Clear chain of authority Quasi-permanent relationships Can direct	Often operates in matrix structure, with low authority Temporary, shared relationships Often must motivate positively
Established organization	Developing and changing organization
Long-term relationships	Short-term relationships
Directs a small set of skills	Directs a diverse set of skills

The selection of a project manager should be based on a number of characteristics. Project managers need flexibility, leadership, confidence, and organizing skills. They should be generalists rather than specialists. They need to communicate well, and to be able to build trust and team spirit. They need general business skills, as well as technical understanding. Project management requires a well-rounded individual.

Team cooperation is critical in projects. Matrix organizations involve high levels of conflict, in large part due to the dual chain of authority found in matrix organizations. Project managers operating in that environment need to function without the authority often found in functional organizations. Within projects, compromise and dealing with conflict in a positive way are usually associated with reduced conflict intensity.

While not always given direct authority, the project manager has control over some resources. The primary source of authority, however, is often the respect gained from professional expertise, and sometimes charm and personality. Professional expertise can be gained from technical knowledge and administrative competence. Some have suggested that project managers try to appear powerful to workers, so that they maximize their influence.

Project managers can be found either inside or outside of the organization. From within the organization, someone with experience and the right specialties is often impossible to find. Therefore, project managers often need to be found from outside the organization. However, this is also problematic, because it takes time to establish alliances and to understand an organization's needs. But usually people with better organizational skills and experience are available in the broader market outside of an organization.

Summary

Information systems projects are very important, providing valuable computer technology for organizations. There is a wide variety of such projects. Web projects tend to involve many similar projects of a short duration. This makes project management easier than the typical kind of information systems project, which may involve a range of time from a month to years, and tends to involve more variety. The largest-scale information systems project is often the installation of an ERP system. This third type of project may be quite short if it simply involves the adoption of a vendor product. However, it can involve many years for global firms revamping their entire information systems support.

Human issues are very critical to the success of information systems projects. Interpersonal conflict may arise due to individual characteristics, team characteristics, project characteristics, or organizational characteristics. The role of each of these areas and how problems in each factor can impact projects was reviewed. Successful project completion requires careful management of each of these factors.

The impact of conflict on performance was reviewed. A little conflict is healthy, reducing the likelihood of complacency and urging us to do more and better things. However, conflict can quickly become counter-productive. It is especially difficult to manage conflict in information systems projects, because there are so many diverse people involved, many of them specialists who deal better with computers than with people.

Projects bring together diverse specialists to work on them. This creates a need for effective communication within project teams. IS/IT projects often involve working with outside organizations, such as vendors and consultants. The need to communicate is the same, but crossing organizational lines can impose additional communications barriers. More formal communication can assure better understanding in this case. There also is a need to communicate with the users that are to be the beneficiaries of IS/IT projects. Communication of all three types needs to be frequent to assure shared understanding in the highly dynamic project environment common to IS/IT projects.

The project manager is central to controlling the project. The project manager must integrate diverse elements to bring projects in on time, within cost, and with satisfactory performance. The project manager needs to be an individual capable of operating with diverse people, and capable of understanding both technical and administrative aspects of the project.

Glossary

Functional manager. Manager of a permanent organization.

Individual characteristics. Result of different personalities, of individuals with different demographic backgrounds as well as education and experience.

Interdependence. People working together, team effort necessary to make projects work.

Interpersonal conflict. Difficulties encountered by people in getting along with others without friction.

Programmers. Information systems job title responsible for building systems.

Project manager. Individual assigned the responsibility of organizing and managing a project.

Project scope. Statement giving project aims and constraints.

Project team. Group of people charged with accomplishing the project through the coordinated efforts of diverse skills.

Systems analysts. Information systems job title responsible for identifying systems needs and designing the software product.

Waterfall model. Prototypical list of systems development activities usually present in an information systems project.

PMBOK Items Relating to Chapter 2

The project manager is the person assigned by the performing organization to lead the team that is responsible for achieving the project objectives.

Project managers have the responsibility to satisfy task needs, team needs, and individual needs.

Project managers accomplish work through the project team and other stakeholders.

An organization's culture, style, and structure influence how its projects are performed.

Organizations are systematic arrangements of persons and/or departments aimed at accomplishing a purpose, which may involve undertaking projects.

Project management success in an organization is highly dependent on an effective organization communication style, especially in the face of globalization of the project management profession.

Organizational process assets are the plans, processes, policies, procedures, and knowledge bases specific to and used by the performing organization.

9.4   Develop project team

9.5   Manage project team

10.1 Plan Communications Management—process of developing an appropriate approach and plan for project communications based on stakeholder's information needs and requirement, and available organizational assets.

10.2 Manage Communications—process of creating, collecting, distributing, storing, retrieving, and the ultimate disposition of project information in accordance with the communications management plan.

10.3 Monitor Communications—ensure that a process providing accurate transfer of information is in place

Thought Questions

1. What are key differences between the job of a project manager and that of a manufacturing plant manager?

2. Identify project success from Gartner Group reports (www.Gartner.com).

CHAPTER 3

Project Organization

Key Points
- Different forms of organization suitable for projects
- Roles of project team members such as liaisons
- Major risk categories (time, cost, quality)

Working on information systems projects will acquaint you with many forms of organization and to many project managers. This chapter reviews the primary types of organization used for information systems projects, and the reasons they are designed that way. The chapter also discusses features desirable in project managers, critical factors in project success.

The purpose of organization is to coordinate the efforts of many to accomplish goals. Organizational structure shows reporting relationships. Figure 3.1 shows a small subset of reporting relationships in a large organization.

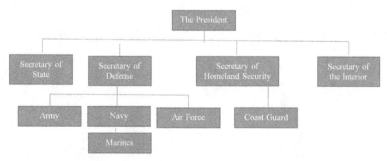

Figure 3.1 Sample organization chart

Alternate Organization Structures

Organization structures represent the hierarchical reporting and official communications networks within organizations. The management hierarchy consists of reporting relationships, an official chain of control or authority. This chain of authority deals with official activities, such as hiring, firing, and promotion. It also includes directing the activities of subordinates. Organizations can be grouped into major subdivisions on the basis of a number of frameworks.

Informal organization can exist in parallel to the official organization structure. Informal organization consists of the network of personal contacts within the organization, and may consist of cliques and groups of people who work well together, and who may not work well with those outside of their subgroup. In organizations with high levels of professionalism (such as in information systems work), informal networks can be very powerful and positive forces. Informal communication is socially motivated. It is very fast, but is not necessarily thorough or dependable. Project managers, as we shall see, have relatively low levels of official authority.

There are three basic forms of project organization: functional, project, and matrix. Each form of organization has its own benefits, and each works well in certain types of environments. The appropriate organization structure depends on the goal of the organization, the type of work it is supposed to do, and the environment within which it operates.

Functional Organization

Functional differentiation organizes elements by specialization (see Figure 3.2). This form of organization relies more on formal rules, procedures, and coordinated plans and budgets to control operations. In a project context, the project is divided into segments that are assigned

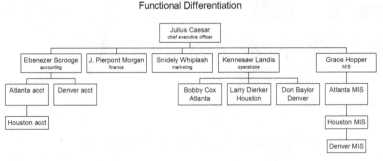

Functional Differentiation

Figure 3.2 Organizational elements by specialization

to the appropriate functional groups, with each functional group head responsible for his or her segment of the project.

Functional organization works well in repetitive, stable environments. Organizational sub-elements are defined by activity or specialty function. All of the accountants in the firm are collected in one location, where they work together. The same is true for the functions of finance, marketing, and MIS. Operations is a separate function, and operational suborganizations are often grouped by geographic location, another optional form of organization. The primary benefit of the functional form of organization is that specialists work together, and can develop professional skills in the most efficient manner. Accountants focus on accounting problems, and become very well trained in accountancy. On the other hand, they gain little exposure to the problems of other organizational elements, such as operations or marketing.

Project Organization

Pure project organization involves creating a separate, independent organization specifically for accomplishing a particular project. One type of example would be the Olympic Committees created to make each Olympic Games work. Once the project is complete, there is no reason for the organization to continue (the next round of games or elections will involve other locations and candidates). Figure 3.3 demonstrates how skills can be grouped by project.

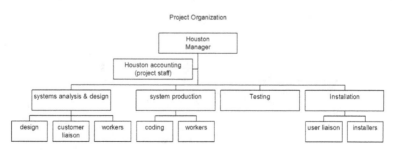

Figure 3.3 Skills grouping

The project center is linked to the parent organization to draw resources and personnel as needed. In the case of Olympic Committees, the permanent International Olympic Committee is available to provide continuity. In the case of committees for elections, there are permanent political parties to draw resources from. Task forces are often announced at a high level, such as the Task Force on Delivery System Reform and Health Information Technology (HITECH) where about $30 billion was invested as part of the Patient Protection and Affordable Care Act. Similar task forces are often created for relocation operations.

Sometimes project organizations are stand-alone organizations. These are newly created organizations for a specific mission, drawn from several organizations. Examples are large-scale public works, like Hoover Dam, or the Dallas-Fort Worth International Airport. NASA space station development drew people from a number of organizations. Often stand-alone joint ventures are used in the construction business for very large projects beyond the scope of participating firms on their own.

Partial project organizations also exist. In this form, the project manager is responsible for some activities, while other activities that are more support oriented, like accounting, remain with functional divisions. This is a common arrangement.

Matrix Organization

If an organization continually operates in a project mode (many organizations do in construction, in information systems, and in consulting), there is a need to quickly create large project groups. The matrix organization form is a grid-like structure of reporting and authority relationships overlaying those of a traditional functional organization (see Figure 3.4).

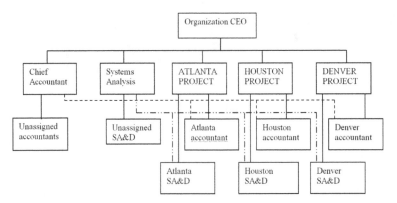

Figure 3.4 Matrix organization

It is used within organizations that make more than minimal use of project teams or product groups. The improved coordination obtained from project organization is combined with the strengths for each specialty that are provided by functional forms of organization. The matrix form of organization was originally adopted by NASA and by the Department of Defense in the 1960s, when contracting practices required contractors to use project management. For each particular project, the contracting firm had to develop a project organization. PMBOK has unique terminology, referring to functional matrix organization as a weak matrix and project matrix form as a strong matrix. These terms are commonly used by those strong advocates of the Project Management Institute.

The key feature of matrix organization is multiple lines of authority. Specialists report to their functional managers with respect to issues involving their specialty, and report to their project managers for specific assignments. Functional specialists are assigned to the project, usually physically located wherever the project is being implemented. But these specialists depend for their personal career decisions on their permanent functional homes. The project accountant works with the project manager, and the project accountant's job is to keep the project manager informed of the cost performance on the project. Since the accountant will work on a number of projects during his or her career, the project accountant's promotion and raises are often decided by the chief accountant at the accountant's permanent organization. Project managers have some input, but the chief accountant would be the project accountant's permanent supervisor. Once the project is completed, the project accountant would return to the organization's accounting office, where he or she would await the next project assignment, or else undertake professional development such as training, or maybe stay with the accounting office on a permanent basis. The same is true of the project engineer. It could be true for the project manager and production personnel as well, although these people often go into the open market to another organization when the project is completed.

Some problems are introduced by the matrix form of organization. The dual reporting structure creates a state of confusion for those who like high levels of structure. It is said that no man can serve two masters. There is also a military principle of unity of command. The matrix system, with two potential sources of direction, has been found to lead to conflict due to incompatible demands and priorities from two managers of a specific individual. Most people are able to cope with such mixed signals, but it causes distress in others. The ability of managers to compromise, and to deal with conflict, has proven very important in project management. While conflict can sometimes lead to improved performance, it needs to be managed carefully. Matrix forms of organizations call upon managers to do a great deal in a difficult environment.

The level of control used within a project organization should vary with the level of difficulty of the problems expected. If there are major technical issues, stronger centralized organization is merited, with a focus on the technical lines of organization. For instance, if a major engineering problem is expected to be critical to the project, engineering components would be centralized under a project engineer. On the other hand, if no major engineering problems were expected, there might not be a project engineer, but rather independent engineers assigned to each work group that needed one. This independence would allow focus on the tasks assigned to the work group rather than overall engineering coordination.

Comparison of Organization Structures in Projects

There are many variations to the three basic organization structures discussed so far in this chapter.

Task Forces

Task forces are temporary groupings of individuals created to solve a particular problem. The task force idea comes from the military, where combining different types of units under a temporary leader for some specific mission is often practiced. In project organizations, individuals with different specialties are grouped together to develop a solution for a specific problem. Long-term task forces can be turned into permanent teams.

Hybrids

Functional matrix and project matrix structures are hybrids of the three basic forms presented above.

A functional matrix organizational structure is used when a project manager is restricted to coordinated functional group assignments. Functional managers are responsible for technical work assignments. The project manager in this case acts as a staff assistant with indirect authority to expedite and monitor project activities.

In a project matrix form of organization, the project manager has more direct authority to decide personnel and work assignments. The functional manager is responsible for providing resources and advisory support to projects.

In the balanced matrix organization, project managers and functional managers have roughly equal authority and responsibility for the project. The project manager typically decides what needs to be accomplished, while the functional managers are responsible for deciding how work will be done and by whom.

Levels of Project Organization

Projects involve a nontraditional form of organization. Traditional organizational design is much more rigid. While no organization is truly permanent, traditional organizational forms are designed on the assumption that they will continue into the foreseeable future. They are not very flexible, and they react slowly to change.

Projects, on the other hand, are organized with the understanding that they are temporary. Some projects can be very long in duration, such as the construction of a cathedral in the 11th to 14th centuries, taking hundreds of years. Other projects may last only weeks, and therefore have very temporary lives. Projects involve very high levels of uncertainty and change, so project organizations need to be flexible and adaptive. In the traditional form, people can enhance their professional training and development. Many organizations that contract to undertake projects typically adopt a functional form of organization for permanent assignments, drawing people for individual projects from their permanent assignments to temporarily work with other specialists on specific projects. This is true in construction, engineering, and large accounting firms specializing in consulting, including information system consulting. Careers with such organizations involve a great deal of relocation as individuals leave their home base for the duration of projects to which they are assigned. Between projects, the organizations may value their specialty skills enough to keep them on the payroll. Ultimately, however, new projects are needed in which these skills can be utilized.

Within project organizations, integrators are often used to facilitate communication. **Liaisons** are used to integrate two groups that are not part of the same organization. Liaisons are especially useful between the people who fund the project and the project team. Project expediters or **coordinators** are individuals whose job is to make sure that something happens. These individuals have no authority, but are assigned to be on top of problems, so that they can inform project managers of the need for additional resources for specific activities.

Criteria for Selection

Table 3.1 outlines the conditions for which a particular organizational form is most often appropriate.

Table 3.1 Comparative organizational forms

Form	Size	Duration	Complexity
Task force	Small to medium	Short to medium	Low to medium
Project team	All	All	Low to medium
Multiple project teams	Medium to large	All	Medium to high
Matrix	Medium to large	All	Medium to high

Other criteria that bear on the project type include uncertainty, cost and time criticality, and the uniqueness of the project. If the project involves high stakes, a matrix form or pure project form gives better control. If there are high levels of certainty, task forces and teams are appropriate because they involve less investment. If time and cost are not critical, task forms and teams are also appropriate. If the project is unique, a partial or full project form is appropriate.

Summary

Organizational structure is a means of achieving goals and responding to problems. Project personnel are often organized into project teams or matrix structures. These organizational forms are more flexible than functional structures that tend to be more bureaucratic. The positive and negative features of alternative organizational forms and their variants need to be understood by top management, so that they can select the organizational form most suitable for their situation. Understanding why these forms exist is also important to those working for them. The matrix form of organization is especially suitable for many projects for large organizations.

Glossary

Coordinator. See Expediter.

Expediter (or coordinator). Individuals who monitor problems in an organization and work on alleviating them rapidly.

Functional organization. Organization by type of work group members do.

Hybrid. Mix between functional and matrix organizational forms.

Liaison. Individual integrating two or more groups through personal communication.

Matrix organization. Grid-like structure of dual reporting relationships combining functional and project organizational features.

Organization. Structure to coordinate efforts of many to accomplish shared goals.

Project organization. Organization by project task or groups of tasks.

Task force. Temporary grouping of people of diverse skills with the intent of accomplishing a specific job.

PMBOK Items Relating to Chapter 3

A project management office is a management structure that standardizes the project-related governance processes and facilitates the sharing of resources, methodologies, tools, and techniques.

Organizational structure is an enterprise environmental factor, which can affect the availability of resources and influence how projects are conducted.

Project governance is an oversight function that is aligned with the organization's governance model and that encompasses the project life cycle.

The composition of project teams varies based on factors such as organizational culture, scope, and location.

9.1 Plan Resource Management—process of identifying and documenting project roles, responsibilities, required skills, reporting relationships, and creating a staffing management plan.

9.3 Acquire Resources—process of confirming human resource availability and obtaining the team necessary to complete project activities as well as material resources.

9.4 Develop Project Team—process of improving competencies, team member interaction, and overall team environment to enhance project performance.

9.5 Manage Team—process of providing guidance and training and applying human resources to tasks.

9.6 Control Resources—process of tracking project human and material resources.

Thought Questions

1. What are the positive and negative features of matrix organization, and why is it often found in project environments?

2. What are the tradeoffs inherent among time, cost, and quality in projects?

PART II

Project Adoption and Planning

CHAPTER 4

Project Selection and Approval

Key Points
- Factors important in project selection
- Project selection methods
- Cost–benefit analysis and net present value
- Multiple objective analysis

The project process begins with a project proposal, generated by users or management. The first step is an initial selection of projects, either on a case-by-case basis, or periodic selection by committees. A related decision of great importance is to keep track of the progress of a project, so that those that are not going to provide value to the organization can be canceled.

Analyzing the expected financial impact of a software project is referred to as a **business case**. Business cases can be accomplished in a number of different ways—some financial, others more subjective; some widely used, some offered as potential improvements. This chapter discusses the decision problem of project selection, and shows how the most commonly used methods work. Analytic methods support this selection process in two ways. First, they provide decision makers with analysis of expected outcomes from adopting specific projects. Second, they provide a basis for communication, so that the reasoning behind a selection decision can be explained to others.

Measurement of Project Impact

Information systems projects typically involve benefits that are difficult to measure in terms of concrete monetary benefits. This vastly complicates sound management, because cost–benefit analysis, the ideal tool for evaluating project proposals, will not always accurately reflect project benefits.

Intangible factors: Both costs and benefits tend to have intangible features. The tangible costs and benefits tend to be historical, backed by data or solid price quotations from vendors. But many of the benefits are expected in the future, and are very difficult to measure. These include expected increases in market share, improved customer service, and better corporate image. These would all have a significant impact on the corporation's bottom line, but guessing exactly what that impact would be is challenging at best.

Hidden outcomes: Other aspects of information technology projects often involve unexpected results. Information technology projects can impact organizational power. New projects can change the power-specific groups may have held in the past, which can have a negative impact on the teamwork of the organization. Information technology also includes components of the organization's communications network. Often different elements of the organization can adopt projects that impact the organizational communications network without this impact being considered. This can result in duplication of efforts, or development of barriers between groups within the organization. Computers can make work more productive and more attractive. But they also can change work roles to emphasize skills in which specific employees have no training, making them feel less productive.

Failure to identify the impact of projects often is not noticed until project implementation. At that stage, the problems created are more difficult to deal with. It is important to consider the systems aspects of projects, and try to predict how the project will change when people do their jobs. Thorough user involvement can make project impact more obvious, as well as easier to reconcile and convince users of the project's benefits.

The changing nature of information technology: There are many excellent applications of computer technology to aid businesses. But a major problem is that technology is highly dynamic. Some information systems projects take years to implement. This can result—and indeed has often resulted—in the installation of a new system after it is outdated by even newer technology.

Selection Practice

Information technology tended to be treated as a capital investment. The following financial techniques have often been used.

1. Payback
2. Discounted cash flow
3. Cost–benefit analysis

Each of these methods will be demonstrated in this chapter. Decision makers treat information technology investment more like operations projects with measurable profitability requirements than the revenue-based appraisals appropriate for training and marketing. Operations investments focus on efficiency-related measures. Conversely, marketing investments are usually viewed in terms of their expected impact on improving competitive position, or increasing market share. The capital approach was very appropriate for hardware proposals, but difficulties were encountered when justifying software. **Intangible benefits** such as competitive advantage or improved practices tended to be disregarded because they are hard to quantify. The most commonly cited justification was reduction in expenses, usually in payroll. The second most common justification involved the subjective aspect of accomplishing some strategic objectives. Intangible benefits cited were enhanced patient care and satisfaction for a health care organization, better speed of responding to customers, and the need to satisfy governmental regulations.

Net present value masks some of the true value of information technology proposals. On the other hand, some projects that have a low impact on corporate performance often appear attractive to cost–benefit analyses. This is because cost–benefit analysis emphasizes those features most easily measured. The value of information technology projects is in making organizations more competitive, increasing customer satisfaction, and operating more effectively. These are sometimes the intangible strategic benefits that are often disregarded because they were not measurable.

Cost–benefit analysis should consider costs over the entire life cycle of the project. Simms stated that life cycle costs are roughly four times those of development costs for most information systems projects. But these long-range costs are much less predictable, and therefore often not included in cost–benefit analyses.

Another issue involves who should do the estimating. In construction, a common practice is to have those who will be responsible for implementing the project do the estimation. This is in a competitive bidding environment, where there is great danger in estimating too low. The motivation is for these estimators to be very cautious. This tends to result in safe estimates considering every possible risk, which is another way of saying that it results in inflated estimates. (Inflating estimates is how you cope with risk at the estimation stage.) In the information systems field, there is far more work to do than the capacity to do it. Therefore, the environment is less competitive. While information system consulting is rapidly growing, in the private sector, competition is based more on negotiation and perceived quality than competitive bidding on price. Therefore, estimators do not have the motivation to consider all risks. Software developers who estimate their own performance tend to be optimistic.

Project Evaluation Techniques

A number of methods exist to evaluate project proposals, either from the perspective of selecting the best option available, designing an ideal option, or rank-ordering options. This section demonstrates some of the most widely used methods, and shows how other methods can be used to consider other factors describing expected project performance.

General Project Selection

Economic and financial analyses include payback (determining the expected time until investment is recovered) and cost–benefit analysis. Net present value and internal rate of return extend cost–benefit analysis to consider the time value of money, appropriate when projects are lengthy (3 years or more).

Checklists describe the criteria of importance and their minimum acceptable levels of requirement. Screening methods are a variant of checklists, eliminating projects that do not have minimum estimated performance on specific measures. Project profiles describe the performance of each project on criteria, so that the decision maker can see each project's strengths and weaknesses. Scoring and rating models are a simple form of multicriteria analysis where measures are obtained on each criterion of importance, and combined in some fashion. Multicriteria decision models are in general more formal than scoring and rating models, but operate on essentially the same principle—identify factors that are important, measure how well each project does on each factor, and combine these into some value score that can be used for ranking.

The rest of this chapter will demonstrate most of the basic methods. The first method demonstrated is screening, a common form of the checklist method that can be and often is combined with other criteria.

Screening

Screening is a process that is very useful in cutting down the dimensions of the decision problem. The way in which screening operates can vary widely in detail, but essentially involves identifying those factors that are important, establishing a minimum level of importance, and eliminating those projects that fail on any one of these minimum standards. Obviously, if the standards are set too high, the decision problem disappears as no projects survive the screening. This is appropriate if the minimum standards reflect what management demands in return for their investment.

To demonstrate screening, assume that 100 information systems project proposals are received this month. All of the projects were evidently worthwhile in someone's mind, but management must consider budgets and other resource limitations. Assume that the criteria and minimum performance levels given in Table 4.1 are required:

Table 4.1 Screening example

Expected return on investment	At least 30%
Qualified project team leadership	Available
Company expertise in this type of work	Either company has experience or desires to gain it
Project completion time	Within 48 months

If any of the 100 proposed projects failed to meet all four of these standards, they would be rejected preemptively. This reduces the number of proposed projects for a more detailed analysis. This approach can be implemented by checklists, which give clearly defined standards on those areas of importance to management.

Screening is good at quickly weeding out those projects with unacceptable features. The negative side of screening is that trade-offs between very good features and these unacceptable features are disregarded. The willingness of decision makers to accept lower return on investment (ROI) for projects with strategic importance is disregarded. For those projects for which such trade-offs are not important, screening is a very efficient way to reduce the number of proposals to a more manageable number.

In the prior section, we gave a list of risk factors for information system projects. These could be implemented as a **checklist** by management specifying minimum acceptable measures that can be used to screen individual projects. Not all risk elements might apply for a given organization's checklist. An example checklist is presented in Table 4.2:

Table 4.2 Example checklist

Factor	Minimum standard
Project manager ability	Qualified manager available
Experience with this type of application	Have experience, or application is a strategically key new technology
Experience with system or language	Personnel with experience can be obtained
Familiarity with modern programming practices	If not, training is available
Availability of critical equipment, software, and programming language	Each critical component available
Project team complete	Key personnel identified and agreed to work; Support personnel easily available

Checklists ensure implementation of policy limits. Checklists are a way of implementing screening from the perspective of what features management feels are important. The next step in analysis is to more directly compare alternative project proposals.

The intent of a **project profile** is to display how the project proposal compares to standards as well as how the project compares to other proposals. Profiles have a benefit over screening limits, because poor performance on one factor can be compensated for by strong performance on another factor. For instance, matching with company strategic programs can be an important factor. There could be other project proposals that contribute nothing to the firm's strategic program, yet have an outstanding cost improvement for administrative work. This would be reflected in very strong performance on ROI. Conversely, another project may have a slightly negative ROI calculation, but may involve entering a new field in which the firm wants to gain experience.

To demonstrate project profiles, assume a firm has a number of information projects proposed. This is generally a large list, because of the many beneficial things information technology can do for organizations. Here we give a short list of six proposals in Table 4.3, measured for resources used, as well as benefits expected.

Table 4.3 Project profiles

Project identifier	Estimated cost	Systems analysts	Cash flow this period	NPV/ Cost ratio	Key to strategy
A265	230,000	3	100,000	0.43	No
A801	370,000	4	−190,000	0.51	Yes
A921	790,000	5	360,000	0.46	No
B622	480,000	3	−52,000	0.11	Yes
B837	910,000	7	−200,000	0.22	Yes
C219	410,000	3	170,000	0.41	No

A profile displays the characteristics of individual projects. Estimated cost is needed to determine if available budget can support a project. The same is true for other scarce resources, such as systems analysts in this case. A tabular form is given above. Graphical displays and ratios are often valuable to give a measure with which relative performance can be measured. For measures such as NPV/cost ratio, cutoff levels can be used to screen out projects. For instance, a 40 percent return on estimated cost in net present terms might be desired. Project B622 and B837 are both below this limit, and might be screened out. However, both of these projects are listed as key to the organization's strategy, and management might be willing to accept a lower return for the potential for advancing organizational strategy.

Traditional Analysis

Assume that a company is proposing an information technology project to improve their operations. They can build the system in-house, or outsource (in effect, installing an over-the-counter, or OTC software product). One year has been allocated to develop and install the system (either in-house or OTC). The benefits of the proposed project are expected to be obtained for 3 years after project completion. Staff will be required to operate the new system. There is some money budgeted to train this staff in the initial year. Staff payroll expenses for this operation include inflation reflected in operating expenses. The company has a marginal value of capital of 15 percent per year.

Cost–Benefit Analysis

The cost–benefit calculation for a new project requires identification of benefits in monetary units. Use of net present value requires identification of the timing of monetary exchanges. The benefit from the new project consists of lowered personnel costs. Calculation of costs and benefits is given in Table 4.4:

Table 4.4 Simple cost–benefit calculation

Year	Develop in-house	Operating cost	Benefit	Net
0	$300,000	$80,000		($380,000)
1		$180,000	$250,000	$70,000
2		$200,000	$350,000	$150,000
3		$225,000	$450,000	$225,000
TOTALS	$300,000	$685,000	$1,050,000	$65,000

Year	Outsource	Operating cost	Benefit	Net
0	$500,000	$20,000		($520,000)
1		$60,000	$250,000	$190,000
2		$80,000	$350,000	$270,000
3		$110,000	$450,000	$340,000
TOTALS	$500,000	$270,000	$1,050,000	$280,000

The outsourced project appears to have a strong advantage in this case. The cost–benefit ratio requires some convention to describe just what costs are assigned to investment and which ones to benefits. Operating expenses seem more appropriately combined with savings, but note that different views might yield opposing conclusions.

Ratio: The nominal cost–benefit ratio (disregarding the time value of money) for the in-house project is $365,000/$300,000 = 1.22. This indicates that the project is worthwhile, in that the extra initial expenses of $300,000 would be exceeded by expected benefits by 22 percent. For the outsourced project, this ratio is $780,000/$500,000 = 1.56. By these measures, the outsourced project appears to have a significant cost–benefit advantage.

Return on investment (ROI) is defined as net project benefits divided by investment (times 100 if you want to view ROI in percentage return). It can be applied to non-discounted cash flows as with cost–benefit analysis. For long-term projects, discounted ROI should be used, which we will demonstrate in the net present value section.

Cost–benefit analysis should consider costs over the entire life cycle of the project. Life cycle costs are roughly four times development costs for most information systems projects, but these long-range costs are much less predictable, and therefore often not included in cost–benefit analyses.

Payback

Payback is a rough estimate of the time required to recover investment. While being simple, payback presents a view of the transaction that is very understandable and important to managers. One alternative may be superior to another on the net present value of the total life cycle of the project. However, cost–benefit analysis does not consider the impact of negative cash flow in early periods. For instance, in our process reengineering example, the cash flow would be as given in Table 4.5. The net benefit column is calculated by subtracting the cost of the new system from the cost of the old system by year. In the first year, this is negative, due to the high investment cost of the new system. In years 2 through 6, the new system provides a positive net benefit relative to the old system.

Table 4.5 Payback

Year	In-house net	Cumulative	Outsource net	Cumulative
0	($380,000)	($380,000)	($520,000)	($520,000)
1	$70,000	($310,000)	$190,000	($330,000)
2	$150,000	($160,000)	$270,000	($60,000)
3	$225,000	$65,000	$340,000	$280,000

Both alternatives gain a nominal advantage by the end of year 3 (pay-back is about 2.7 years for the in-house alternative, about 2.2 years for the outsourced alternative). However, $380,000 has been sacrificed at the beginning for the in-house alternative and $520,000 for the outsourced alternative. One of the most common reasons for company failure in the United States is lack of cash flow. In this case, if the firm has cash-flow difficulties, the outsourced option would be less attractive than if they had adequate cash reserves.

Net Present Value

We can modify the cost–benefit ratio by considering the **time value of money**. In this project, for instance, the nominal expected gains of $1,050,000 are spread out over 3 years, while the development costs are incurred at the beginning. Having the $380,000 (or $520,000 for the outsourced alternative) would mean that the company would not be able to adopt some other investments (and maybe even force the firm to borrow money). The marginal value of money for the firm is 15 percent per year. **Net present value** converts a time stream of money back to its worth in today's terms (or in terms of the project's start, or any other specific time of reference).

Table 4.6 shows the changes in cash flow between the two systems (shown in the net difference column). Discounting each year's net change in cash flow by the discount rate of 1.15 per year to the t-th power, where t is the time period, we get the following. Note that initial expenses are treated as occurring during year 1.

Viewed in this light, relative to obtaining a return of 15 percent per year on alternative investments, adopting the in-house alternative would be like writing a check initially for over $57,000, while the outsourced alternative would be equivalent to a gain of over $72,000.

Table 4.6 Net present value

Year (t)	In-house net	Divide by 1.15^t	Outsource net	Divide by 1.15^t
0	($380,000)	($380,000)	($520,000)	($520,000)
1	$70,000	$60,870	$190,000	$165,217
2	$150,000	$113,422	$270,000	$204,159
3	$225,000	$147,941	$340,000	$223,556
NPV		($57,768)		$72,932

A related concept is **internal rate of return** (IRR), which is the marginal value of capital for which the net present value of a stream of cash flow would break even, or equal zero. Note that IRR can equate to ROI in that ROI is viewed with discounted cash flow. In this case, the IRR amounts to 1.07 for the in-house alternative, for 7 percent average return, while the IRR of the outsourced alternative is 1.225, or an average return of 22.5 percent. By these measures, the outsourced alternative is attractive and the in-house alternative is not.

Cost–benefit analysis seeks to identify accurate measures of benefits and costs in monetary terms, and uses the ratio benefits/costs (the term benefit–cost ratio seems more appropriate, and is sometimes used, but most people refer to cost–benefit analysis). For projects involving long time frames, considering the net present value of benefits and costs is important.

Other Factors

There are a number of complications that can be brought into the calculation of cost–benefit ratios. One of the most obvious limitations of the method is that benefits, and even costs, can involve high levels of uncertainty. The element of chance can be included in cost–benefit calculations by using expected values. For instance, the demand for production output appears to be increasing. Therefore, using an expected demand of 30,000 units per year is probably conservative. Demand could very well continue to increase. The expected value calculation can be quite complicated in its purest form, consisting of identifying all possible demands for a given year and associating accurate probabilities to each outcome. Instead of getting involved in such a speculative and detailed exercise, most managers do what we did—assume a conservative value. However, it should be recognized that there is added benefit to the new machine in its ability to expand. If this expansion capacity is not considered in the cost–benefit calculation, the new machine option is not accurately evaluated.

For instance, if growth in demand was expected to increase at the rate of 1,000 units per year, this form of benefit for the new machine could be reflected as follows, where an extra ($2 - $1.20) × 1,000 units/year = +$800 in gain is obtained each year. As before, net difference is calculated as the new machine cash flow minus the old machine cash flow. Table 4.7 shows the calculations.

Table 4.7 Net present value calculation

Year (t)	Old machine	New machine	Net difference	Divide by 1.15^t
0	0	-$100,000	-$100,000	-$100,000
1	$6,000	$24,000	+$18,000	+$15,652
2	$6,000	$24,800	+$18,800	+$14,216
3	$6,000	$25,600	+$19,600	+$12,887
4	$6,000	$26,400	+$20,400	+$11,664
5	$6,000	$27,200	+$21,200	+$10,540
6	$6,000	$28,000	+$22,000	+$9,511
7	$6,000	$28,800	+$22,800	+$8,571
8	$6,000	$29,600	+$23,600	+$7,715
9	$6,000	$30,400	+$24,400	+$6,936
10	$6,000	$31,200	+$25,200	+$6,229
NPV				+$3,921

This would involve a cost–benefit ratio in net present value terms of $103,921/$100,000 = 1.04, and an ROI of 1.160, greater than the company cost-of-capital of 15 percent.

The cost–benefit ratio does not reflect intangible benefits unless they are presented in monetary terms. Cost–benefit analyses have included measurements for intangible items, but they tend to be given lower values because of the uncertainty involved in their estimates. Detailed analyses of the decision maker's willingness to pay for intangible factors have been conducted, but can be time-consuming and less than convincing. Governments have encountered some problems in applying cost–benefit analysis to public works, to include (1) evaluating the benefit of recreational facilities and (2) placing a dollar value on human life. When a dam is built, there clearly is benefit obtained from providing many citizens much improved fishing and water sports. (There is also added cost in depriving citizens of the opportunity to view some flooded historical sites.) The approach usually taken has been to place some dollar value on recreation, based on some very insubstantial measures. The evaluation of human life has also been tackled by economists, who have applied things like the net present value of the expected earnings of those whose lives are expected to be lost in some proposed investment project. This of course involves high levels of speculation as well, because the calculation assumes certain ages, assumes that the only value of a human is what they earn, and disregards who pays and who benefits.

If a firm was threatened with a severe monetary penalty for not complying with a governmental regulation with respect to environmental pollution or safe working conditions, a net present value analysis might well lead to the conclusion that it would be rational to pay the penalty and avoid improving operations. For instance, assume that a blast furnace is pouring out black matter at a phenomenal rate that the government finds terribly offensive. Governmental regulations call for a penalty of $10,000,000 if the pollution source is not cleaned up within 1 year. Hard-core cost–benefit analysis would identify the cost of cleaning up the facility, which might involve an expense of $12,000,000 in equipment and installation, and an added cost of operations of $5,000,000 per year over the next 8 years, the remaining life of the equipment. At a discount rate of 12 percent per year, the net present value of benefits and costs would be as shown in Table 4.8. The net column shows discounted values for benefits and costs. Totals are presented in the end.

Here the ratio of net present benefits to net present costs is $8,928,571/$35,552,483 = 0.25, well below 1.0, indicating that the rational decision maker would pay the fine and keep operating as is. But the government did not impose the fine limit for the purpose of raising money. They imposed the fine as a means to coerce polluters to clean up operations. The U.S. Congress has no trouble adding extra zeroes to penalties. If the firm continued to pollute, it is not too hard to imagine

Table 4.8 Net present value calculation

Year	Benefit	Net	Costs	Net
1	$10,000,000	$8,928,571	$17,000,000	$15,178,571
2	–		$5,000,000	$3,985,969
3	–		$5,000,000	$3,558,901
4	–		$5,000,000	$3,177,590
5	–		$5,000,000	$2,837,134
6	–		$5,000,000	$2,533,156
7	–		$5,000,000	$2,261,746
8	–		$5,000,000	$2,019,416
Total		$8,928,571		$35,552,483

the penalty being raised in the future to a much larger figure. There have been actual cases similar to this scenario, where within 3 years the penalty was raised to much larger values, providing a much different cost–benefit ratio. Benefits are often difficult to forecast.

To demonstrate intangible benefits in our machine investment case, one of the clear advantages the new system has is in its higher level of quality output. The loss of discarded products is included in the analysis. But poor production quality results in more than just the identification of products not passing testing limits and rejecting them. Quality comes on a continuous scale. The older machine will in all likelihood include the production of a number of products that barely pass test limits, and do not contain desired levels of quality. The customer will accept them, but slowly over time a reputation for inferior workmanship will result. The new machine should improve the company's image with respect to quality. Placing a dollar value on image is pure speculation. Rigorous proponents of cost–benefit analysis would disregard such benefits that are immeasurable as "soft," and not worthy of hard-core analysis. Managers with more vision would recognize that there was a relative advantage for the new machine that was not reflected in the cost–benefit analysis.

An additional benefit of the new machine is that it is more flexible. It has the capacity to respond to larger markets because it has added capacity. At the moment of analysis, there is only one customer. We have just considered the impact of increased demand on the part of this customer, but there might be additional sources of sales in the future. This again would be highly speculative. A hard approach would require the decision maker to identify a specific expected increase in demand. A soft approach would list flexibility as a measure of importance. There could also be other advantages that are intangible, such as the safety of workers, impact on market share, or replenishing capital equipment, so that old facilities do not fall apart, disrupting the ability of the firm to conduct business.

Multiple Objectives

Profit has long been viewed as the determining objective of a business. However, as society becomes more complex, and as the competitive environment develops, businesses are finding that they need to consider multiple objectives. Although short-run profit remains important, long-run factors such as market maintenance, product quality, and development of productive capacity often conflict with measurable short-run profit.

Conflicts

Conflicts are inherent in most interesting decisions. In business, **profit** is a valuable concentration point for many decision makers because it has the apparent advantage of providing a measure of worth. Minimizing **risk** becomes a second dimension for decision making. There are cash flow needs, which become important in some circumstances. Businesses need **developed markets** to survive. The impact of advertising expenditure is often very difficult to forecast. Yet decision makers must consider advertising impact. **Capital replenishment** is another decision factor which requires consideration of trade-offs. The greatest short-run profit will normally be obtained by delaying reinvestment in capital equipment. Many U.S. companies have been known to cut back capital investment to appear reasonably profitable to investors. **Labor** policies can also have an impact on long-range profit. In the short run, profit will generally be improved by holding the line on wage rates and risking a high labor turnover. There are costs that are not obvious, however, in such a policy. First, there is training expense involved with a high turnover environment. The experience of the members of an organization can be one of its most valuable assets. Second, it is difficult for employees to maintain a positive attitude when their experience is that short-run profit is always placed ahead of employee welfare. And innovative ideas are probably best found from those people who are involved with the grass roots of an organization—the workforce.

This variety of objectives presents decision makers with the need to balance conflicting objectives. We will present the simple multi-attribute rating technique (SMART), an easy to use method to aid selection decisions with multiple objectives.

The **simple multi-attribute rating technique (SMART)** method offers a simple way to quantify subjective elements. There are two elements to the value function in SMART: factor weight (w_i) and score (s_{ij}) of each alternative j on each factor. Overall value is then:

$$value_j = \sum_{I=1}^{K} w_i \times s_{ij}$$

Weights w_i can be obtained in a number of ways, but a simple estimate with some reliability involves ranking the factors, considering the range of likely performances, and then estimating the relative value of moving from the worst to the best performance relative to such a swing from either the most important or the least important. We will do both, and use a rough average of these two estimates. In the example used earlier in this paper, assume that the ranges and rankings for the five criteria are as given in Table 4.9.

Table 4.9 Criteria weight development

Criterion	Worst	Best	Rank	Best = 100	Worst = 10
Risk	Very high	Very low	2	70	120
Market share	Very negative	Very positive	1	100	150
Control	Low	High	5	5	10
Investment	$1,000,000	$100,000	4	25	40
Return (NPV)	0%	100%	3	50	80

First, the extreme expected measures for each criterion are identified, for the decision maker to understand the range of possibilities to compare. Then, the decision maker ranks the importance of swinging from the worst measure to the best measure for each criterion. In this case, the decision maker considered it most important to move market share impact from very negative to very positive, followed by moving risk from very high to very low, moving expected return from 0 percent to 100 percent, investment from $1 million to $100,000, and finally (and least important) moving control from low to high. Next the decision maker is asked to quantify these changes. Viewed from the perspective of the most important criterion, if changing market share impact from very negative to very positive were worth 100, the decision maker assigned a value of 70 to risk, 50 to return, 25 to investment, and 5 to control. To get a second estimate, with 10 assigned to the least important criterion (control), the assigned values were 40 for investment, 80 for return, 120 for risk, and 150 for market share. This information is then used to generate the set of weights w_i. Each of the sets of assigned weights is totaled, and each entry divided by the appropriate total. This gives two estimates of weights, which the decision maker can use to compromise (preferably using rounded numbers) as in Table 4.10.

Table 4.10 SMART calculation of weights

Criterion	Best = 100	Divide by sum	Worst = 10	Divide by sum	Compromise
Risk	70	0.28	120	0.30	0.29
Market share	100	0.40	150	0.375	0.39
Control	5	0.02	10	0.025	0.02
Investment	25	0.10	40	0.10	0.10
Return (NPV)	50	0.20	80	0.20	0.20

The scores (s_{ij}) for each alternative on each criterion are now needed. These can be assigned directly, to reflect any kind of utility function for each criterion. Better performance should always receive a higher score than an inferior measure. A possible set of assigned scores are given in Table 4.11.

In this case, the outsourced alternative has a clear advantage.

Summary

We have reviewed some of the primary methods used to evaluate project proposals. Screening provides a way to simplify the decision problem by

Table 4.11 SMART value calculation

Weights	0.29	0.39	0.02	0.10	0.20	1.00
Criteria	Risk	Mkt Share	Control	Invest	NPV	Values
In-house	0.1	0.5	0.9	0.8	0.1	0.342
Outsource	0.8	1.0	0.3	0.6	0.9	0.868

focusing on those projects that are acceptable on all measures. Profiles provide information that display trade-offs on different measures of importance. Cost–benefit analysis (with net present value used if the time dimension is present) is the ideal approach from the theoretical perspective, but has a number of limitations. It is very difficult to measure benefits, and also difficult to measure some aspects of costs accurately. One way of dealing with this problem is to measure more accurately. Economists have developed ways to estimate the value of a life and the value of scenic beauty. However, these measures are difficult to sell to everybody.

A more common view is that it is wasted effort to spend inordinate time seeking a highly unstable and inaccurate dollar estimate for many intangible factors. Value analysis is one such alternative method. Value analysis isolates intangible benefits from those benefits and costs that are more accurately measurable in monetary terms, and relies upon the decision maker's judgment to come to a more informed decision. The SMART method, one of a family of multiple criteria decision analysis techniques, provides a way to quantify these intangible factors to allow decision makers to trade-off values.

Cost–benefit provides an ideal way to proceed if there are no intangible factors (or at least no important intangible factors). However, usually such factors are present. Intermediate approaches, such as payback analysis and value analysis, exist to deal with some cases. More complex cases are better supported by multiple criteria analysis. In cases of constraints, such as budgets, it is sometimes appropriate to optimize over some objective. Linear programming provides a means of generating the best portfolio of funded projects subject to constraint limits given that accurate measures of project performance are available.

Glossary

Business case. Financial analysis of a proposed information systems software project.

Checklist. A means of evaluating initial project proposals in terms of a list of expected characteristics.

Cost–benefit analysis. Economic analysis pricing all factors, dividing benefits by investment.

Discounted cash flow. Conversion of cash flows into their worth as of some base period, usually the present.

Intangible factors. Items of value that are difficult to quantify in monetary terms.

Internal rate of return. The marginal value of capital that yields a net present value of zero for a stream of cash flow.

Multiple criteria analysis. Analysis considering not only one measure of value (such as profit), but the value trade-offs over multiple measurement scales.

Net present value. The worth, in today's terms, of a stream of cash flow over time, assuming a given marginal cost-of-capital.

Optimization models. Models of decisions allowing the identification of the decision that is optimal with respect to selected criterion (or criteria).

Payback. Financial analysis estimating the time required to recover investment.

Project Profile. A display of expected project performance on important criteria, allowing a comparison of alternative projects.

Return on investment (ROI). Rate of financial return on investment, defined as net profit divided by investment.

Screening. A method of implementing a checklist for project evaluation by listing the worst acceptable performance on a list of criteria.

SMART. Simple multi-attribute rating theory, a means of objectively comparing the values of projects considering multiple criteria.

Tangible benefits. Benefits that are measureable; in cost–benefit terms, measurable specifically in monetary terms.

Time value of money. The current worth of future flows of cash flow.

PMBOK Items Relating to Chapter 4

Business value is defined as the entire value of the business.

All projects can be mapped to the generic project life cycle structure of start, organize and prepare, carry out, and close.

A project phase is a collection of logically related project activities that culminates in the completion of one or more deliverables.

4.2 Develop Project Management Plan—map out how the project is to be accomplished.

7.1 Plan Cost Management—process that establishes the policies; procedures; and documentation for planning, managing, expending, and controlling project costs.

12.1 Plan Procurement Management—process of documenting project procurement decisions, specifying the approach, and identifying potential sellers.

12.2 Conduct Procurements—process of obtaining seller responses, selecting a seller, and awarding a contract.

Thought Questions

1. Compare the ease of estimating costs and benefits of projects with estimation of costs and benefits in repetitive operations. Why might they be different?

2. Cost–benefit analysis is cited as the ideal method for economic analysis in some circles. What are the limitations and/or issues with cost–benefit analysis?

3. Describe a few multiple criteria that typically are involved in projects.

CHAPTER 5

Systems Development

Key Points
- Definition of requirements analysis
- Waterfall and other methods for systems design
- The Capability Maturity Model (CMM)

There are seemingly unlimited proposals for implementation of computer systems to aid organizations. Every time one of these proposals is adopted, it creates the need for an information systems project—to bring an application online. Project management is one of the most important developing areas in information systems. It is difficult to bring an information systems project to completion on time, within budget, and meeting specifications. There are many citations of the scope of this problem. A partner of KPMG, Peat Marwick, said that, on the basis of a survey of 250 companies, some 30 percent of information systems projects exceeded the original budget and time frame by at least a factor of 2, or did not conform to specifications. A report issued by The Standish Group reports industry statistics every year, but these statistics are very stable. Only around 15 percent come in on time and within budget. For large companies, the success rate is closer to 10 percent. It was also reported that only about 40 percent of planned features and functions end up in the final version of the software. Over half of the software development projects initiated by large companies cost nearly 200 percent more than the original estimation. Yet information systems projects offer great value for companies.

To develop systems efficiently, a methodology needs to be applied. Organizations use a wide variety of methodologies. The purpose of this chapter is to provide an overview of traditional systems development methodologies. It is becoming more and more important to apply continuous improvement standards to the processes used within businesses. Standards such as ISO 12207 (disseminated originally in 2008) and Software Engineering Institute's Capability Maturity Model (CMM) focus on improving the processes of software development. Software development organizations are being required by some user organizations to certify compliance with these standards. Compliance is also very beneficial to software-producing organizations. We will review these standards. Types of information systems projects and their features are examined, followed by a broad framework of the systems development approach.

Requirements analysis identifies the data and information needed to automate some organizational task and to support the achievement of organizational objectives. Many information systems failures have been attributed to a lack of clear and specific information systems requirements. Accurate identification of requirements early in the process has been reported to result in successful systems and lower costs for error correction.

Requirements analysis can consist of four processes:

- conceptual design
- logical design
- validation
- formal specification

Conceptual design is the process of developing a model of what the system should do. Critical factors such as the implementation environment, organization goals and policies, product and service flows, and anticipated problems need to be identified.

The **logical design** process is where the strengths and weaknesses of the conceptual design are assessed. Organizational and technological factors both have to be considered. Organizational factors include resources required, organizational politics, and priorities. Organizational factors are better understood by viewing projects as systems collecting interacting components with a common purpose. Technological factors refer to existing systems capabilities, the availability of needed data, and the availability of needed personnel. The logical design process is a system design considering the organization's strengths and weaknesses.

Validation is a process meant to ensure that a valid set of requirements has been developed. Features that need to be considered in the validation process include data entry methods, system outputs, and other impacts of the proposed project on the overall system.

The **formal specification** is the result of requirements analysis. The statement of work and business case can be used to document the project in terms of its intended mission. An ideal formal specification clearly specifies a complete set of information requirements, to include inputs and outputs, and what these elements are to do.

This process then culminates in the project sponsors creating a project **charter**, a formal authorization for work to proceed. The formal specification focuses on project technical matters. The project charter can be used for the organizational budgetary process to enable activity to proceed within proper control of authorized stakeholders. The charter includes a detailed description of the project in the form of project **scope**, which defines what will be included in the project.

Overview of Analysis and Design Methods

There are a number of approaches that traditionally have been used to analyze and design information systems projects. The laissez faire "code-and-fix" model, where code is written and problems are fixed, resulted in many problems when it came to implementation, and fixing was often expensive.

The Waterfall Model

The waterfall model recognizes feedback loops between stages of software development to minimize rework, as well as incorporating prototyping as a means to more thoroughly understand new applications. The waterfall model (named because each step follows its predecessor in sequence) consists of the following stages, each of which can involve reversion to the prior stage if attempts at validation uncover problems. The waterfall model (Table 5.1) has the advantages of encouraging planning before design, and decomposes system development into sub-goals with milestones corresponding to the completion of intermediate products. This allows

Table 5.1 The waterfall model of software life cycle stages

Stage	Feedback determinant
System feasibility	Validation
Software plans and requirements	Validation
Product design	Verification
Detailed design	Verification
Code	Unit test
Integration	Product verification
Implementation	System test
Operations and maintenance	Revalidation

project managers to more accurately track project progress and provides project structure.

The list shown is for a software life cycle product. Variations in the stage labels are used for different types of projects, such as acquisition of software, implementation of a vendor system, or other kinds of projects. Each stage involves a test, either validation or verification. Validation is the process of evaluating software to ensure compliance with specification requirements. (Is this the right product?) Verification is the process of determining whether or not the software component functions correctly. (Is the product built right?)

In the original waterfall model, problems accumulated over stages and were not noticed until project completion, resulting in very expensive code. User needs were often not met, resulting in a rejection of products after they were built. Therefore, feedback loops were added, along with prototyping to catch problems early. The waterfall model does not allow a rapid response to the pervasiveness of change in information systems projects. The orderly sequence of activities in the waterfall model does not accommodate new developments. Some systems, especially those involving higher levels of uncertainty and with less investment at stake, are often designed and built using more flexible development methods, such as rapid prototyping, object-oriented process, or rapid application development.

Prototyping is the process of developing a small working model of a program component or system with the intent of seeing what it can do. Thus, it is a learning device, appropriate especially for users who are not absolutely sure of what they want from a system. Prototyping can be a valuable part of the waterfall approach.

Prototyping

When dealing with systems that involve beneficial features that are difficult to both predict and price, the systems development approach has proven ineffective. The hard, clear dollar benefits rarely are sufficient to justify adopting the system.

A prototyping approach involves building a small-scale mock-up system, allowing the user to try it out. The user could then ask for modifications based on a better idea of what the system could do. Prototyping is a much less thoroughly planned approach, but is often appropriate for applications with low investment and low structure. This can result in much lower development cost and time, especially when there is a lack of clarity on what a user wants from a system.

Prototyping is very useful in leading to a greater understanding of project requirements by definition. It has also been found to improve design effectiveness, because users are directly integrated into the design process in a manner that they clearly understand. Prototyping is not appropriate for all types of system developments. However, for smaller scale systems, prototyping is a very effective means of demonstrating what proposed systems would be able to do.

Agile Software Development

A response to the poor performance record of information systems with respect to time, budget, and functionality, some in the software industry have developed collaborative techniques to develop software much faster and closer to user requirements. These techniques are known as agile methods, and include a number of versions. However, the common bases for these techniques include working closely with users throughout the project, iteratively developing software versions in the spirit of prototyping, demonstrating these prototypes to users to identify required changes in direction, and avoiding heavy documentation in favor of getting software developed faster.

Agile methods have proven very effective when applied to small projects. They also work (with care) for larger projects, although effort is needed to get teams to work well together. The best case is when a small, self-organized, and motivated team located in the same location works with a small number of on-site customers. There are even cases when teams have worked in a geographically separated environment, although synchronization of efforts is required.

The economy in recent years has had a major impact on the software industry. Because of the increased importance of bringing software products to the market faster, a revision of traditional methods has been apparent. Agile methods are techniques of software development designed to deliver these products faster, with more functionality necessary for users.

There are many different techniques that have been used in this effort to attain agile programming. These include collaborative techniques (pair programming, having customers work on-site as team members). What this amounts to is working quite closely with customers to ensure that the software products developed are exactly what the customers needed. For instance, a common agile practice is to have customers write acceptance tests. This approach emphasizes that:

- Focus on individuals and their interactions is preferred over a focus on processes and tools.
- Delivering working software is more important than comprehensive documentation.
- Customer collaboration is sought rather than contract negotiation.
- Response to change is preferred to following plans.

The agile approach maximizes cooperation with users that has been found to be so critical to information systems project success. The principles behind the agile movement are:

- Highest priority is given to satisfy the customer through early and continuous delivery of valuable software.
- Requirement changes are welcomed, even late in the development process. Agile processes harness change with the aim of improving customer competitive advantage.

- Working software is delivered frequently, from a couple of weeks to a couple of months, preferably to shorter timescales.
- Cooperative work between business people and developers is needed on a daily basis.
- Projects are built around motivated individuals, who operate in a positive environment with all the support they need, and who are trusted to get the job done.
- Face-to-face conversation is relied upon as the most efficient and effective method of communication.
- The primary measure of progress is working software.
- Agile processes promote sustainable development.
- Technical excellence and good design are sought continuously, enhancing agility.
- Simplicity is essential.
- Self-organizing teams develop the best architecture, requirements, and designs.
- Teams reflect on ways to become more effective at regular intervals, and tune and adjust behavior accordingly.

The agile approach is often combined with other methodologies in hybrid forms.

Other Options for Systems Development

Many projects are developed from scratch, applying conventional systems development approaches. In the following iterative life cycle approaches, tasks are performed on a crash basis to meet tighter time goals.

- **Component assembly projects**: typically object-oriented modules for use in a variety of other applications
- **Rapid application development**: techniques to compress the life cycle, to include computer-aided software engineering (CASE) and Joint Application Development (JAD). CASE tools involve a degree of reuse of previously developed systems. To complete projects on an accelerated timescale, project objectives and scope need to be identified early, and joint development of user requirements

must be effective. Group systems, as discussed in Chapter 3, may be of use in this type of application. Care must be taken in assigning team members on a full-time basis, and heavy user participation is very important. Rapid application development can lead to reduced development time, lower development cost, greater user and employee satisfaction, and lower ultimate maintenance costs. However, it is appropriate for small projects, and not those involving significant levels of complexity.

Software Development Standards

Quality improvement has been an area of major development in the operations management area. One of the key ideas involved is that of continuous improvement—developing a philosophy of business in which the way in which work is done (processes) is continuously reviewed with the intent of improving them. This emphasis on the quality process has been widely implemented in the United States in the annual Baldrige Award competition, as well as the European Quality Award Assessment Model. Two other programs which have had a major impact in the software development industry include ISO 9000 (European standards for production and management processes) and the Software Engineering Institute's CMM.

The Software Engineering Institute's **Capability Maturity Model** includes five levels of maturity. These are shown in Table 5.2, along with actions generally required to move from one level to another. Organizations that have done nothing to improve their software development methods are assigned to level (1), and are considered to involve high levels of risk and a focus on survival.

Moving from the initial level (1) to level (2) requires instilling basic discipline in people management activities. This is accomplished through adopting software management approaches.

Moving from level (2) to level (3) requires that organizations identify the primary competencies required in processes, and taking action to make sure that the people assigned to these activities have these competencies. This can be done through training or hiring. Processes are defined and institutionalized in level (3) organizations.

Table 5.2 Capability maturity model features

Level	Features	Key processes
1. Initial	Chaotic	Survival
2. Repeatable	Individual control	Software configuration management Software quality assurance Software subcontract management Software project tracking and oversight Software project planning Requirements management
3. Defined	Institutionalized process	Peer reviews Intergroup coordination Software product engineering Training program Organization process definition Organization process focus
4. Managed	Processes measured	Quality management Process measurement and analysis
5. Optimized	Feedback for improvement	Process change management Innovation involving technology Defect prevention

Moving from level (3) to level (4) requires the quantitative management of organizational growth in human management capabilities, and establishment of competency-based teams. Process measurement and analysis needs to be implemented.

Moving to the highest level requires the continuous improvement of methods adopted to develop personal and organizational process abilities. In this state, greater technology innovation is expected by some. All expect better defect prevention.

Projects accomplished by organizations at various levels for a typical 500,000 line (500 kLOC) software project have been studied. The results dramatically indicate the benefits of attaining higher levels of capability maturity, as shown in Table 5.3.

It is clear that adopting capability maturity principles pays. Level 1 projects are expected to take far longer (thus costing far more). They also have much inferior quality as measured by defects. Implementing the CMM requires significant investment, effort, and discipline. However, it is clearly better than the *ad hoc* state of doing nothing.

Table 5.3 Capability Maturity Model Integration (CMMI) effectiveness

Level	Development cost $ million	Development time Months	Product quality Defects/kLOC	LOC/h
1	33	40	9	1
2	15	32	3	3
3	7	25	1	5
4	3	19	0.3	8
5	1	16	0.1	12

Systems Development Approach

The systems development approach provides a rational way to evaluate information systems projects. The systems development approach is based on a complete life cycle analysis. Project proposals evaluated by this approach are measured on cost, time, and performance. **Cost** is concerned with resources being spent as expected. Accurate budgets and benefit estimates are needed to accurately evaluate proposals. They also provide valuable control mechanisms during project implementation. **Time** is a critical variable in projects. First, it is highly correlated with cost. Second, delayed benefits are worth much less than early benefits, due to the time value of money. Keeping a project on schedule is a major challenge. **Performance** is a critical third measure. Projects need to perform to specifications and user requirements.

Later, when the project is being implemented, these measures are critically important. Performance needs to be ensured through quality testing. Time is a major means of evaluating how well the project is progressing. We will later look at Gantt charts as a means of planning the time dimension of projects. Cost budgets are also critically important in controlling project implementation. Because of the high levels of uncertainty inherent in projects, management must closely monitor project progress, and be prepared to shift resources and replan activities as required.

System life cycles consist (in broad terms) of the activities of specification, design, coding, data conversion, testing, and implementation. These activities tend to be serial, although data conversion can proceed in parallel with coding.

Specification

Projects start with somebody's problem. Computer systems are powerful tools that solve many problems. Therefore, there are many times when they offer improved means of doing things.

Once a proposed application is identified, a systems analyst who understands how to build such systems needs to be obtained to plan a solution. The systems analyst needs to start by talking to the people that proposed the application to find out what they want, and to the people that are budgeting the project to find out the constraints in terms of costs that need to be considered. It is best to discuss the proposed project with all groups affected, so that something is not designed that will be counterproductive or create unexpected problems. After these interviews, a clearer statement of the problem should be developed. An effective way to proceed is to identify alternate solutions, and to determine the costs and expected performance features of each, so that the budgeting authority can select the best system possible. A **feasibility study** is a clear, concise statement of the problem, followed by a detailed formal description of the current system describing the problem. Adequate qualitative and quantitative information should be provided to determine whether the effort should be continued. The elements and components of the proposed system are identified.

The specification phase should provide a clear problem statement of what the system is intended to do, with a rudimentary idea of a systems solution. Once the initial authorization is obtained, the system is defined in greater detail. A **statement of work** specifies what is to be done. This needs to specify new system objectives, and provide measures for the acceptability of the system upon completion. Performance objectives should not be constrained by the existing system. One approach that works well is to start with general objectives. Objectives should include sub-elements that are measurable. This phase of the systems development approach results in a comprehensive list of activities, along with their schedules, costs, and required resources. This includes hardware and software requirements. When presented with the costs of proposed systems, many are rejected. It is in the specification phase that most projects die.

Design

The design phase develops how software will meet requirements. One of the classic business analyses is the decision to **make or buy**. This decision is very pertinent to computer systems, because there are many vendors that produce and sell many useful computer systems. Every organization has the option of buying products from vendors, or of building the product themselves. In general, buying products from vendors is a much lesser hassle. But you have to live with the features that the vendors put into the product. They make a living telling everyone that this is exactly what they need. In truth, it often isn't. Furthermore, even if it is, vendors may charge more than the product is worth. But building products in-house requires a lot more risk and time. If required expertise is not available, it may well be worth spending a little more on the vendor. Usually the vendor route is faster, and quite often it is cheaper. The problem usually lies with matching the existing system, and doing the job required.

Recently, it has become very popular to hire large portions of information processing, or to **outsource**. One purpose of outsourcing is downsizing. Many functions can be outsourced, including data center management, telecommunications, disaster recovery, and legacy systems maintenance. This avoids the need to waste scarce resources, and can gain efficiencies by hiring vendors with expertise. Outsourcing can also be used for the company's Internet operations. If plans are clearer, Internet functions that could be outsourced include connectivity, Web server hosting, firewall security, website development, and content development. These activities are complex, subject to change, and not particularly relevant to organizational core competencies. Outsourcing makes sense when a fast start-up is important, internal skills are lacking, and the vendor can provide strong features. Outsourcing for Internet operations is not as worthwhile if they are of strategic importance to the business, or requirements are ill-defined. Rarely is outsourcing used for all tasks that a project entails. A need for internal training to implement the system and to integrate it with the existing system will arise for some tasks.

If vendors or outside contractors are being considered, a **request for proposal** is required including the feasibility study and the plan for project development. The request for proposal states the user requirements in terms of system objectives, project scope, and performance specifications as well as constraints, especially in terms of time. It is necessary to develop a qualified bidders list of those with the ability to accomplish the work required.

The project team needs to be selected at this stage. The project manager should be selected, to suit certain characteristics, which we will discuss later. Team members should be drawn from functional areas. Functional managers should be sold on the project, so that good team members are obtained.

The output of the design stage is a detailed list of user requirements and system requirements. Tasks are broken down into work packages, and team members are given specific assignments. The project manager is responsible for setting up schedules, budgets, and controls. The output of the design stage is a task breakout, with each task scheduled by date. It is necessary to continue close coordination between the systems analyst, the ultimate user of the system, and the budget authority. A project never is completely designed, nor finally adopted, until it is complete. A very accurate understanding between the analyst, user, and owner is necessary to develop systems that are useful and cost-effective.

Code (or Acquisition)

Options, in-house or vendor, need to be evaluated. If in-house, the conventional phase of coding to implement the design is applied. If options including purchasing the products or services of a vendor are adopted, the term acquisition seems more appropriate. Whatever option is adopted, project sponsors should conduct a **business case** (financial analysis, which in projects should consider risk).

If outside vendors or contractors are being considered, selection of the bidder to build the project (or project components) involves some options. There are a number of bases for selecting a bidder. If the system quality has been thoroughly defined to the extent that every bidder has the knowledge and if each bidder has been screened to ensure their competence, selection on the basis of a low bid is usually used. This has obvious advantages, using the competitive system, to lower costs. However, selecting the low bidder has obvious risks if the bidder is not truly qualified. In fact, in some parts of Europe, the winning bidder is the one closest to the average bid, using the logic that they must know what they were asked to do. Regardless, there are other considerations besides the low price.

- Cost—need to ensure that it is within the allowable budget
- Feasibility—need to ensure that the bidder can actually do the project
- Experience—look at the bidder's record on similar projects
- Reputation—bidder's record with respect to quality work

Oftentimes, if the bid is too high, the user can negotiate with the bidder. Ethics are involved if an open competitive bidding process was used. Those not selected may not have been treated fairly if the rules are changed after the initial bid. However, in the private sector, this is a legal way to proceed, and the owner and the bidder can work together to negotiate an acceptable agreement for both. Negotiation is appropriate especially when dealing with complex systems when it is attractive to share risks.

In-house systems development begins with the design stage, which involves converting specifications from the definition phase into plans. The proposed system is broken down into subsystems, components, and parts. All elements need to be checked for compatibility, as well as for their ability to meet specifications. Prototyping can be used if there is benefit from seeing what the system will look like.

The system is developed and whatever hardware and software is needed is procured. The system is constructed, and any code and interfaces that are needed are programmed. System testing is conducted concurrently with the assembly of the system to catch errors as quickly as possible. Development of training materials is often accomplished concurrently as well.

Production of a system follows analysis and design as it can involve a large group of diverse people, from programmers, people building user interfaces, people designing the database interfaces, people dealing with the users to design reports, and people to set up any required networks for multiple users. The project manager must consider availing people with the right skills at the right time, obtaining needed facilities in terms of tools and places to work, realistic time estimates allowing for the appropriate level of uncertainty, and of course capital. Quality testing should be accomplished throughout production. It is a good practice to build systems in modules, and thoroughly test each component before adoption. If at all possible, it would be best to include the user in this testing.

Testing

Quality control is very important throughout the system development cycle. Each module needs to be checked before a block of work is considered complete. Organizations usually have independent testing groups assigned to review system components to ensure that they are capable of dealing with the expected workload.

Implementation

Once the system is satisfactorily built and tested, it is moved from the builder to the user. This requires that the system be installed and checked out to ensure that it does what was specified. Training the users with technical support available once the system is turned over to the user wraps up the project cycle. The user evaluates system performance and if any flaws are detected, the builder would fix them. Sound contractual agreements spelling out procedures before starting the project are very useful at this stage. Builders often provide maintenance support for systems, usually at a nominal fee. The operation phase includes system improvement.

Summary

Many systems and analysis methods have evolved to support information systems projects. The different methodologies discussed in this chapter all have important roles to play for software projects with specific environmental conditions. Each organization tends to adopt a particular methodology. It is not as important which methodology is adopted as it is that a methodology be adopted. It is also important that software-producing organizations adopt process standards. The SEI/CMM has proven to be dramatically effective at improving process quality and productivity.

Systems development needs to consider cost, time, and performance in addition to specific criteria of importance to a specific project. The activities by system stages were reviewed.

Glossary

Agile software development. Methodology emphasizing speed, with a focused team working intensely to bring out a software project to meet an ambitious deadline.

Business case. Financial analysis of a project proposal.

Capability maturity model. Carnegie Mellon rating system for organizational software development maturity.

Charter. Formal document authorizing organizational support for a project.

Data warehousing. Large-scale database technology to organize and store vast quantities of data, enabling data mining analysis.

Decision support systems. Computer systems used to evaluate alternative decision choices.

Enterprise resource planning. Systems designed to provide all organizational MIS needs through integrated, optimized computer software.

Feasibility study. Analysis prior to adoption of a project intended to determine whether the system is doable, within a prescribed budget.

Formal specification. Documentation of project mission and scope.

Implementation phase. Phase of an information systems project where the finished product is put into operation.

Informatics. Business analytics in a contemporary environment, potentially involving access to big data analyzed by machine-learning software.

Internet commerce. Doing business over the Internet.

Make or buy decision. Selecting the alternative among making an information systems element with in-house resources, or purchasing the element from a vendor.

Management control. Use of information systems to control an organization.

Outsourcing. Hiring others to do at least part of one's information system.

Process. Activity undertaken to accomplish something the organization needs done.

Prototyping. Testing of a system by developing a small-scale model, so that it can be evaluated.

Rapid prototyping. Use of prototypes with user feedback to quickly identify system weaknesses.

Request for proposal. Formal document outlining project requirements to prospective vendors, asking for their product and associated price.

Scope. Detailed description of the project and/or product, part of the project charter.

Specification phase. phase of an information systems project where specifications are generated based on requirements analysis.

Statement of work. Formal document specifying standards for a computer software project.

Systems analysis. Function of identifying what an information systems project is intended to do.

Systems design. Result of computer software project design intended to accomplish elements identified in systems analysis.

Systems development approach. Rational way of systematically evaluating information systems projects.

Transaction processing. Use of computer systems to perform repetitive clerical tasks for an organization.

Validation. Process of ensuring that the software performs as designed.

Waterfall model. Systems development cycle consisting of serial activities.

PMBOK Items Relating to Chapter 5

4.1 Develop Project Charter—the process of developing a document that formally authorizes the existence of a project and provides the project manager with the authority to apply organizational resources to project activities.

4.2 Develop Project Management Plan—establish processes needed to accomplish the project and their interrelationships.

4.4 Manage Project Knowledge—establish a process to communicate information needed to control the project.

5.1 Plan Scope Management—process of creating a scope management plan that documents how the project scope will be defined, validated, and controlled.

5.2 Collect Requirements—conduct requirements analysis from stakeholders.

5.3 Define Scope—develop detailed description of the project and product.

5.4 Create WBS—develop the list of activities needed to accomplish the project.

5.5 Validate Scope—process of formalizing acceptance of the completed project deliverables.

5.6 Control Scope—concretely establish project boundaries.

Thought Questions

1. Compare the waterfall methodology with agile approaches.

2. Describe how the CMM system works in project environments. What are the benefits of using it? What are the associated costs?

CHAPTER 6

Agile Project Development

Key Points
- Description of agile approaches to project development
- Related systems, to include scrum and lean techniques

A response to the poor performance record of information systems with respect to time, budget, and functionality, some in the software industry developed collaborative techniques to develop software much faster and closer to user requirements. These techniques are known as agile methods, and include a number of versions (scrum, extreme programming, lean techniques). However, the common bases for these techniques include working closely with users throughout the project, iteratively develop software versions in the spirit of prototyping, demonstrating these prototypes with users to identify required changes in direction, and avoiding heavy documentation in favor of getting software developed faster. While agile techniques might seem the reverse of the Capability Maturity Model approach, a number of Level 5 software producers have been found to use agile techniques when faced with stiff schedules and budgets for important projects.

PMI View of Agile

The Project Management Institute (PMI) publishes its Project Management Body of Knowledge (PMBOK) regularly, seeking to standardize project management concepts and practice. The PMI views a project as a temporary group of activities designed to produce a unique product, service, or result. PMBOK provides rules, guidelines, and characteristics for project management, viewing project management as a process divided into the groups of:

- Initiation—define and authorize the project
- Planning—define project scope, and plan needed actions to reach the goal
- Execution—train people to follow the project management plan
- Monitoring and control—during project evolution, identify needed corrective actions
- Closing—formal acceptance by owner and project conclusion

These process groups are supported by PMBOK knowledge areas:

1. Project integration management—activities needed to coordinate a group of processes and their activities
2. Project scope management—activities guaranteeing that the project covers all planned elements
3. Project time management—activities guaranteeing project conclusion in planned time
4. Project cost management—plan, estimation, budgeting, and control of costs to accomplish the project
5. Project quality management—determination of responsibilities, objectives, and quality policies
6. Project human resource management—management of the project team
7. Project communication management—generation, collection, distribution, storage, and recovery of data
8. Project risk management—identification, monitoring, analysis, and proposed solutions to manage risks
9. Project procurement management—purchase and supply of products and services required

The PMBOK seeks to provide a general structure applicable to all projects. In practice, this can be found to be bureaucratic and rigid. Agile approaches were intended to overcome some of these limitations, although it must be noted that formal approaches do have benefits in well-established project environments where change is less common.

Agile Definition

Agile is a project management ideology providing a lightweight alternative to the waterfall approach of systems analysis and design. Agile was intended to be more responsive, relying on close working relationships among teams dealing with specific development components.

Agile methods have proven very effective when applied to small projects. They also work (with care) for larger projects, although effort is needed to get teams to work well together. The best case is when a small, self-organized and motivated team located in the same location works with a small number of on-site customers. There are even cases when teams have worked in a geographically separated environment, although synchronization of efforts is required.

Differences between agile and traditional (waterfall model) systems development are demonstrated in Table 6.1.

Conforto et al.[2] administered questionnaires to 19 Brazilian firms involved with projects in new product development, in part motivated by an examination of the idea that agile methodology could be applied outside of the software industry. Literature review was used to identify agile project management practices, to include:

Table 6.1 Comparison of agile with traditional project development[1]

Factor	Traditional model	Agile
Management style	Process (command and control)	People (leadership/ collaboration)
Assignments	Individual	Team
Communication	Formal (hierarchical)	Self-organizing (open)
Development model	Lifecycle	Evolutionary iterative
Organizational structure	Mechanistic (matrix, project)	Organic (participative team)
Team location	Often distributed	Collocated
Documentation	Substantial—before project start	Less—interactive input during project
Resource utilization	Optimize plan	Ad hoc
Customer involvement	Requirement analysis	Continuous
Cost estimation	Initial	Guess in each sprint
Quality control	At end of phases	Continuous
Contractual issues	Clear initial definition	Estimates evolve

- Focus on product vision
  It was found that those using the agile approach had minimal textual description, followed by more detail at the end.
- Use of simple project planning and communication tools and processes
  Those applying the traditional approach used Gantt charts or work breakdown structure, as opposed to less formal tools like spreadsheets or visual panels, pictures, or drawings.
- Use of iterative planning
  Those firms using the traditional approach applied more detailed project planning.
- Frequent monitoring of planning and updating processes
  Those firms using the traditional approach applied detailed planning with revision, while the agile firms developed by iteration.
- Activities developed (and monitoring and updating) by self-managed teams

Traditional firms updated the project plan at the end of each phase. Agile firms updated weekly.

The economy in recent years has had a major impact on the software industry. Because of the increased importance of bringing software products to market faster, revision of traditional methods has been apparent. Agile methods are techniques of software development designed to deliver these products faster, with more functionality necessary to users.

There are many different techniques that have been used in this effort to attain agile programming. These include collaborative techniques (pair programming, having customers work on site as team members). What this amounts to is very closely working with customers to ensure that the software products developed are what customers needed. For instance, a common agile practice is to have customers write acceptance tests.

This approach emphasizes:

- Focus on individuals and their interactions over focus on processes and tools.
- Delivering working software is more important than comprehensive documentation.

- Customer collaboration is sought rather than contract negotiation.
- Response to change is preferred to following plans.

This manifesto clearly diverges from the principles of the Capability Maturity Model. However, the agile approach maximizes cooperation with users that has been found to be so critical to information system project success. The principles behind the agile movement are:

- Highest priority is given to satisfy the customer through early and continuous delivery of valuable software.
- Requirement changes are welcomed, even late in the development process. Agile processes harness change with the aim of improving customer competitive advantage.
- Working software is delivered frequently, from a couple of weeks to a couple of months, preferably to shorter timescales.
- Cooperative work among business people and developers is needed on a daily basis.
- Projects are built around motivated individuals, who operate in a positive environment with all the support they need, and who are trusted to get the job done.
- Face-to-face conversation is relied upon as the most efficient and effective method of communication.
- The primary measure of progress is working software.
- Agile processes promote sustainable development.
- Technical excellence and good design are sought continuously, enhancing agility.
- Simplicity is essential, seeking to maximize the amount of work not done.
- Self-organizing teams develop the best architecture, requirements, and designs.
- Teams reflect on ways to become more effective at regular intervals, and tune and adjust behavior accordingly.

Agile emphasizes team performance. Thus attention should be given to team composition and building teams that work well together. Thus conflict resolution is important. The method emphasizes working together and collocation, diverging from a recent tendency in information technology of distributed teams.

Stakeholder engagement is also important, with focus on the total quality management concept of delighting customers. This requires a thorough understanding of stakeholder needs to build a shared vision across the development team. Creativity needs to be fostered, along with strong communication with stakeholders by applying critical interpersonal skills.

Agile calls for progressive elaborations of project development. Problems, risks, threats, and issues need to be uncovered and understood to develop sound solutions. Decisions should be made at the last responsible moment to consider all important factors.

The outcome of agile project management includes the project and team charter, backlog preparation and refinement, and activities to include stand-up, retrospective, and demonstration reviews. Performance needs to be measured to enable troubleshooting. Agile provides a means to intensively develop products and is useful when creativity needs to be emphasized and time is a factor. Traditional approaches work better for larger-scale projects.

Scrum

The scrum approach is one form of agile development approach, focusing on performing work in short iterations, usually from a week to a month. During these periods (time-boxes), sprints occur where a cross-functional team performs all tasks (such as design, building, and testing) needed to complete a working feature. Scrum teams usually involve 6 to 10 members providing cross-functionality. One team member is the product owner representing the stakeholders. There also is a ScrumMaster, a coach, facilitator, and remover of impediments. Each sprint involves meetings, to include planning (identification of issues and their prioritization), stand-ups (daily meetings where team members describe what they have accomplished and plan on doing next), reviews, and retrospectives.

The relative advantages of agile and traditional software development approaches (waterfall) have been compared.[3] The traditional approach was perceived as ineffective in software project management, as project releases were often late as well as failing to meet client requirements. Part of the problem is that clients have minimal interaction with the project team, at which time the clients often do not have a clear idea of what they want. Agile software development follows a project plan, but without great initial detail. Plans are designed in stages iteratively. The focus is on completing projects faster and at a lower cost.

The scrum methodology is structured around the components of **roles**, **artifacts**, and **processes**:

Roles—the three key roles are the scrum master, the product owner, and the scrum team. The scrum master provides loose team leadership, and interacts with the environment. The product owner sets the scope of the project and prioritizes product requirements, constantly refined as the project progresses. The scrum team is self-organized and builds the product in sprints (iterations).

Artifacts—the product backlog consists of prioritized project requirements, and provides a road map. After the product backlog is completed, the scrum team breaks it into sections of work, creating the sprint backlog. Progress is constantly monitored and time estimates are updated daily. These estimates can be plotted, creating a burn-down chart, showing daily estimates of time remaining. User stories are stored as sprint backlog items. These stories consist of an ID, name, importance, initial estimate, demo procedure, and notes. User stories are sorted into smaller tasks for teams to complete.

Processes
1. Kick-off—project launch
2. Sprint planning meeting—determine sprint backlog and objectives—all attend
3. Daily scrum meeting—Scrum master and team spend about 15 minutes to track progress and identify issues and delays
4. Sprint review meeting—held after a sprint to demonstrate functionalities—all attend
5. Retrospective meeting—after sprint review meetings, scrum master and team identify problems experienced and evaluate backlog, as well as develop ways to improve future sprints
6. Interruptions—lead to requirements changes

Agile has been proposed for smaller firms. Scrum has been proposed as workable for large firms as well. Scrum has project risk management features, with product owner meetings providing a forum for risk consideration in backlog development, while daily team communication, scrum meetings, and sprint planning give means to identify and mitigate risks.

Kanban

The kanban approach has been applied in lean manufacturing for decades (Toyota factories in the 1940s and thereafter), credited with improving quality by immediate detection and correction of problems, with residual benefits of reducing clutter by controlling work in process (WIP) and inventory by ordering materials to arrive just in time. Kanban is another agile methodology that has been applied to software development projects (and by inference can be applied to other projects. In kanban, roles are not prescribed. Signals of work process are used to limit WIP.

Workflow visualization—work is divided into specific tasks, visualized in columns on a board, indicating its state in the workflow

Limiting WIP—explicit limits to the number of tasks are defined for each workflow state

Measuring lead time—defined as the time from task creation to completion—measured to optimize workflow and to make it as fast and predictable as possible

Table 6.2 shows a comparison of scrum and kanban agile methodologies: Scrum splits work into small tasks, accelerating completion, and major backlog items, making it suitable for software projects. Kanban splits work into even smaller items to ensure a continuous work process, not using the concept of sprints. Both methodologies work on items by prioritizing, allowing product release immediately upon completion. This makes the kanban approach highly suitable for customer service environments.

Summary

Agile practices provide a means to rapidly develop projects, providing a platform conducive to creativity. It works if teams work closely together in a spirit of collective ownership. Team leaders need to develop and

Table 6.2 Comparison—Scrum and Kanban[4]

	Scrum	Kanban
Iterations	Sprints	None
Product release	At end of each sprint, at owner discretion	Constant development
Teams	Cross functional	Specialized
Roles	Product owner, Scrum master, team	None prescribed
Change management	Changes at the beginning of new sprints	Prompt response to any change
Meetings	Planned	None required
WIP	Limited per sprint	Limited per workflow state
Product backlog	Listed prioritized items	Board cards
Visualization	Board, product backlog, sprint backlog	Board to visualize the process
Bottleneck management	Addressed immediately	Avoided

maintain a close collaborative working environment. The process includes daily meetings with a demonstration of features emphasized, and documentation delayed until the product takes firm form. Agile needs full stakeholder participation, and operates in the spirit of just in time.

Glossary

Agile. Project management approach streamlining project execution to obtain quicker project completion.

Artifacts. Documents describing product backlog.

Capability maturity model (CMM). Carnegie Mellon Institute system of software development functionality standards widely used to assess organizational software development process capability.

Kanban. Agile lean manufacturing approach.

Project Management Body of Knowledge (PMBOK). PMI set of standards comprehensively covering project management processes.

Scrum. Project management approach focusing on short iterations of work to gain quicker project completion.

Work in process (WIP). Partially completed inventory—in the context of project management, the number of tasks defined for a project.

PMBOK Items Relating to Chapter 6

6.1 Plan Schedule Management—establish activities needed for agile implementation of the project.

Thought Questions

1. Compare agile, scrum, and lean approaches to waterfall methodology.
2. Try to find evidence of success or failure in agile project applications.

Notes

1. Sundararajan, Bhasi, and Vijayaraghavan (2013).
2. Conforto et al. (2014).
3. Tanner and Mackinnon (2015).
4. Yordanova and Toshkov (2019).

PART III

Project Completion

CHAPTER 7

Risk and Schedule Delay

Key Points
- The impact of delays in projects
- Allocation of relative responsibility for delays

We have contended that projects are often (in fact usually) late, due to the complex interaction of activities with probabilistic durations. This has been found to be true in many repetitive project environments to include construction as well as software system development projects.

In the construction industry, delay types, or allocation of blame (owner versus contractor, or acts of nature), is often important. Delay types are also categorized as excusable (compensable or noncompensable) and nonexcusable. Project delay has received a great deal of attention in civil engineering.[1]

There are several techniques comparing as-planned and as-built schedules reviewed by Alkass et al. (1996).[2]

1. Global impact
2. Net impact
3. Adjusted as-built critical path method (CPM)
4. "But-for" or collapsing
5. Snapshot
6. Time impact

The global impact technique plots all delays and disruptions on a bar chart, with start and finish dates for each event determined. Total project delay is calculated as the sum of durations of all delaying events. The issue with this approach is that the effect of concurrent delays is disregarded, and delay types are not differentiated as every delay has an equal impact, resulting in an overstatement of entitlement as liability.

The net impact technique displays only the net effect of all claimed delays on a bar chart of the as-built schedule. Time extension is the difference between the as-planned and the as-built completion dates. This method also does not differentiate the type of delay and the true effect of a particular delay on overall project completion is difficult to determine.

The adjusted as-built technique uses a CPM format for the as-built schedule, displaying delays as activities linked to work activities. Critical paths are identified using the as-planned schedule, and again using the as-built schedule. The net effect on project completion date is again used. Again, however, delay types are not considered.

The "but-for" technique is also called a collapsing technique, using the CPM format. One party takes the as-planned schedule and inserts all delays that they accept responsibility for. The updated schedule yields a revised project completion date, which is compared with the as-built schedule, implying that this party is responsible for this much delay. The as-built schedule is calculated from both owner and builder perspectives.

The snapshot technique gives a means to determine the amount of delay in a project, when it occurred, and its causes. Total project duration is divided into time periods (snapshots), often coinciding with major project milestones. The project completion of this extended schedule is compared with the as-planned schedule, determining delay. Then the causes of delay are assessed. This approach is systematic and objective, but involves significant effort.

The time impact technique is similar to the snapshot technique, examining effects of delays at different project times. As opposed to the snapshot technique, the time impact technique concentrates on specific delays, not time periods. This method also takes significant effort, and requires analysis to apportion entitlement.

The "but-for" approach seems the most straightforward. Usually a contractor has a penalty to pay for being late. The "but-for" contractor schedule is a way to show a fair and reasonable finish time given no contractor fault. It is possible that a management firm is the agent for the owner, in which case responsibility needs to be allocated across the two entities, and the "but-for" schedules for both contractor and manager can be compared, and serve as input to the negotiations to assess relative penalty.

Demonstration Schedule

The following case is widely used in civil engineering publications. The project consists of ten activities (A through J) with the following durations and precedence relationships (Table 7.1).

Table 7.1 Kraiem and Diekman CPM data

Activity	Planned duration (days)	Actual duration(days)	Predecessors
A	7	11	-
B	5	10	-
C	7	12	A
D	9	9	B
E	6	15	B
F	4	6	C
G	3	5	D
H	9	11	E
I	5	12	F
J	3	5	H

This yields the planned schedule shown in Figures 7.1 and 7.2.

	1	2	3	4	5	6	7	8	9	10	11	12	13	14	15	16	17	18	19	20	21	22	23	Pred
A																								-
B																								-
C																								A
D															S	S	S	S	S	S	S			B
E																								B
F																								C
G																		S	S	S	S	S	S	D
H																								E
I																								F
J																								H

S – slack

Figure 7.1 Planned schedule

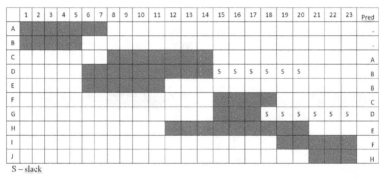

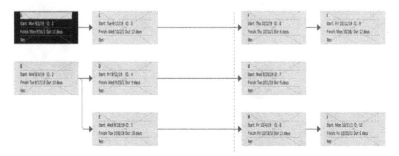

Figure 7.2 Network diagram of planned schedule

Delays are categorized as excusable noncompensable (EN)—nature, excusable compensable (EC)—manager's responsibility, and nonexcusable (NE)—contractor's responsibility. In the example, delays by activity and category are given in Table 7.2.

Table 7.2 Demonstration of project delays

Activity	EN delay—excusable	EC delay—manager	NE delay—contractor
A	1 day		3 days
B	3 days	1 day	1 day
C		2 days	3 days
D			
E	5 days	3 days	1 day
F		2 days	
G		1 day	1 day
H	1 day	1 day	
I	2 days	2 days	3 days
J	2 days		

Figure 7.3 gives the bar chart for this project, beginning at an arbitrary starting time on September 2, 2019.

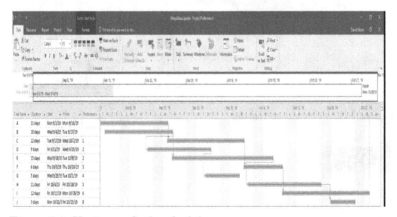

Figure 7.3 Kraiem as-built schedule

These delays result in the as-built schedule shown in Figure 7.4.

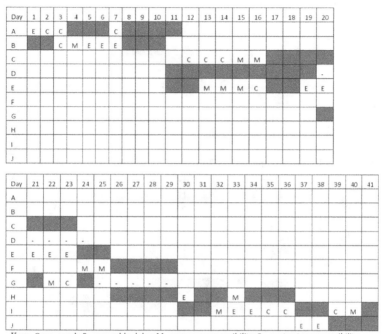

Key: Gray — work; E — excusable delay; M - manager responsibility; C — contractor responsibility

Figure 7.4 As-built schedule

This as-built schedule is 18 days later than the planned finish time of 23 days. We can create the "but-for" schedule to show what would have happened but for delays due to management by taking out the "M" delays, obtaining the "but-for" schedule from the perspective of the contractor (Figure 7.5).

Figure 7.5 shows that but for the delays that were the responsibility of management, the contractor would have finished the project in 36 days. The argument would thus be that the contractor is responsible for 13 days of penalty rather than 18. If there is joint responsibility to be considered, the "but for" schedule from the perspective of the management firm is shown in Figure 7.6.

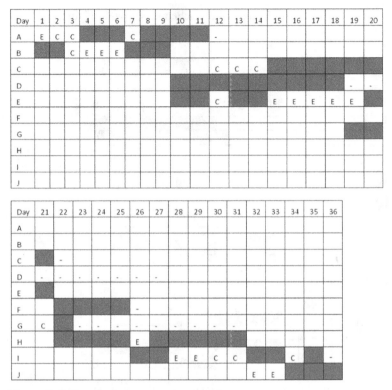

Figure 7.5 But-for contractor perspective

Here we see that the delays due to contractor responsibility taken out result in project completion time of 39 days. This is 16 days late. There is an overlap of 13 days, with the management firm responsible for the extra 3 days.

Such an exercise usually involves exercise of negotiation skills, arguing over who is responsible for what. This exercise generally starts with the project participants, but often then extends to the involvement of lawyers, and if that is not resolved, courtrooms.

Summary

Schedule delay is usually present in projects. Contracts are usually written to cover contingencies. The material in this chapter demonstrates some methods that might be utilized to reconcile delay responsibility in an equitable manner. But ultimately, the analysis usually will be material upon which lawyers can base their arguments.

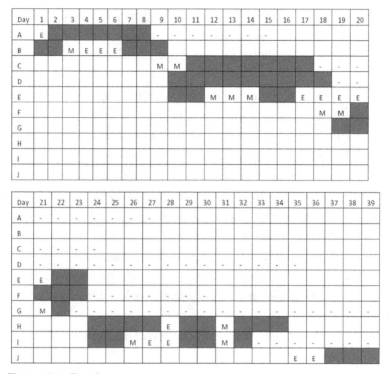

Figure 7.6 But-for manager perspective

Glossary

As-built. Schedule that actually occurred.

But-for. Schedule that would have occurred but for delays for which one party is responsible.

Compensable. Delay for which one party to the contract is liable to the other party.

Excusable. Delay for which the entity (owner or contractor) is not liable.

Nonexcusable. Delay for which fiscal liability is present.

PMBOK Items Relating to Chapter 7

8.1 Plan Quality Management—process of identifying quality requirements and/or standards for the project and its deliverables and documenting how the project will demonstrate compliance with quality requirements.

8.2 Manage Quality—process of auditing the quality requirements and the results from quality control measurements to ensure that appropriate quality standards and operational definitions are used.

8.3 Control Quality—process of responding to quality issues identified.

11.1 Plan Risk Management—process of defining how to conduct risk management activities for a project.

11.2 Identify Risks—process of determining which risks may affect the project and documenting their characteristics.

11.3 Perform Qualitative Risk Analysis—process of prioritizing risks for further analysis or action by assessing and combining their probability of occurrence and impact.

11.4 Perform Quantitative Risk Analysis—process of numerically analyzing the effect of identified risks on overall project objectives.

11.5 Plan Risk Responses—process of developing options and actions to enhance opportunities and to reduce threats to project objectives.

11.6 Implement Risk Responses—process of dealing with risk issues as they arise.

11.7 Monitor Risks—process of auditing project quality performance.

Thought Questions

1. Describe the definitional differences between excusable and nonexcusable delays.

2. Describe the system of conflict resolution for projects, ending with the means of last resort.

3. Discuss how project risk can be dealt with.

Notes

1. Kraiem, Z.M., Diekmann, J.E. (1987). Concurrent delays in construction projects. *Journal of Construction Engineering Management* 113(4), 591–602.

2. Alkass, S., Mazerolle, M., Harris, F. (1996). Construction delay analysis techniques. *Construction Management and Economics* 14, 375–394.

CHAPTER 8

Project Implementation

Key Points
- Categories of project failure
- Primary reasons for project failure
- Definition and role of a project champion

In this book, we began with a discussion of the risks involved in accomplishing a project. We then discussed what is involved in information systems project development. We now return to an overall perspective of what is involved in the final implementation of projects, with the intent of examining things that can be done to improve a project's prospects of success.

Project Success

Not all projects fail. Care to involve users early in the requirements analysis has proven to be very effective in information system projects. Although there was inevitable variance in the computer literacy of users, the comprehensive and carefully planned training program for the implementation of the new corporate-wide information system led to the successful adoption of a more efficient and flexible system.

Project Failure

There are many cases of projects failing, for a variety of reasons. The implementation stage involves putting the system developed by the project into operation, and turning the system over to the user. For information systems projects, the major elements of implementation are system installation and conversion, user acceptance testing, and user training. If testing procedures are cut short as a means of recovering lost time, catastrophic failure often results.

Many projects fail to some degree in terms of meeting design specifications or meeting time and cost estimates. Most project problems are not apparent until late in the project.

Technical validity refers to the system accurately doing the job it was designed to do. Organizational validity has to do with people using the system. Systems can be technically valid, but if there are reasons why users will not use them (such as difficulty in using them), the system will have been a waste. Organizational effectiveness refers to how the system contributes to better performance by the organization. Information system elements are meant to lead to better decision making, but the quality of decision making is impossible to measure except in very narrow contexts. Profit is often used as a measure of effectiveness, but rarely is only one factor responsible for changes in profitability. Probably the best measure of information system effectiveness is its use. Those systems that are used probably are successful, but even those may involve problems.

Four major categories of project system failure are:

- Corresponding failure
- Process failure
- Interaction failure
- Expectation failure

Corresponding failure alludes to the failure of the system to meet design objectives. This is a technical failure in that a computer code did not do what it was intended to do.

Process failure is a failure to bring in a project system on time and within budget. The system may technically work, but it is no longer economically justifiable, or at least not within current business plans.

Interaction failure occurs when a system is not used as much as it was planned to be. This can arise when a system is built to technical specifications within budget and on time, but the intended users do not use it. This can be because of some bias on the users' part to continue to operate the old way, or because the planned system design really did not effectively deal with the problem.

Expectation failure occurs when the system does not quite match up with the expectations of project stakeholders. The system may perform technically, and may be on time and within budget, and may be used, but may not do the job as management was led to expect.

Primary Reasons for Project Failure

Surveys of reasons for project failure consistently identify user involvement as the primary reason, followed by lack of top executive support, and lack of clear statement of business objectives. While these factors are specific to information systems projects, they have a lot of similarity to failure reasons in any project. These traditional critical success factors continue to be cited as the most important.

Lack of Client Involvement

Heavy involvement on the part of users is needed for project success for two important reasons. First, systems analysts need user input to accurately identify the business system, and what business problems are. Second, the project will not work if users do not use the computer system. If the users have been involved in identifying computer system problems, and have been consulted about proposed solutions, there is a much greater likelihood that they will accept the project.

Lack of Top Management Support

Projects have a very difficult time succeeding if they are not "fostered" by top management. Project leadership is important too, but favorable views at the top, with control over purse strings, are probably more necessary for projects to succeed.

That is not to say that support within the project team is not important as well. The implementation team needs to develop team building and cooperation to succeed. Successful team characteristics include a clear sense of mission, understanding of interdependencies of system elements, cohesiveness of the system, and shared enthusiasm and trust within the project team. Within project teams, it is necessary to be flexible. It is also necessary to keep everyone informed.

Although there is no one best leadership style, project managers should have the ability to motivate and inspire. This in great part is due to the fact that they have little coercive authority, especially within matrix organizations.

In addition to the project manager, another key role is the project champion. Project champions often have no authority, but are crucial to the success of projects. A comparison between project managers and champions is given in Table 8.1.

Table 8.1 *Comparison between project managers and champions*

Project manager	Project champion
Technical understanding	Cheerleader
Leadership and team building	Visionary
Coordination and control	Politician
Obtain and provide support	Risk taker
Administrative	Ambassador

Project champions have been found to be crucial at maintaining interest in information systems projects. This can be very positive, but it can also be negative if counterproductive projects are kept alive after their need has passed. This also has occurred when strong project champions have been present.

Lack of Project Definition

A detailed project plan needs to be developed, defining the system, user requirements, and system requirements. Part of this plan is a clear statement of the business objectives of the proposed system.

The system definition should identify the project team, including its leaders. Team members should be drawn from functional areas. Networks of the flow of information should be developed, along with identification of tasks and their relationship. Budgets need to be established and policies need to be stated.

User requirements include performance measures. These measures are needed to determine the acceptability of the final product. For legal reasons, as well as for operational continuity, it is wise to have good documentation. This documentation becomes the ultimate reference for resolving issues that arise during the project.

Quality Control in Project Implementation

Implementation planning involves developing plans and gathering resources to install the system and train users. **Quality control** is an important element in implementing the project.

One reason that reported losses on information systems projects are so high is that many projects are canceled late in the project's life. This is because most problems are not identified until the testing stage of a project, after much of the cost of the project has been expended. Boehm[1] provided relative estimates of the cost of defect removal. For large projects, the ratio of removing defects by phase was estimated to be as shown in Table 8.2.

Table 8.2 Relative defect impact

Stage	Relative cost of defect removal
Requirements definition	1
Design stage	3.5
Coding stage	10
Testing stage	50
After delivery	170

It is obvious that correcting errors at an early stage is far better than later. To identify errors at early stages, early testing is required. High levels of quality in any operation are obtained by quality inputs, careful production, followed by testing in realistic environments, and user feedback.

Actual installation of information systems can be accomplished in a variety of ways. Alternative strategies include parallel installation, pilot operation, and cold turkey approaches. **Parallel installation** involves running the new system in parallel with the old system. This is the most expensive approach, because the resources required to operate both systems are used. However, it is far safer than other approaches. The **pilot operation approach** involves running the new system on a limited basis. This does not expose the system to a full load. Obvious problems can be identified by this pilot approach, but problems due to workload will not be detected. The **cold turkey approach** is to place a great deal of faith in the new project, pull the plug on the old system, and turn on the new system. This approach is not recommended if it can be avoided.

Summary

Four levels of project failure were presented. Studies of both information system project failure and success were reviewed, intending to identify the circumstances that led to failure, and using these bad experiences to identify procedures that can reduce the likelihood of failure. Additionally, a number of studies of information systems project failure were reviewed.

The primary causes of information system failure are lack of user involvement, lack of top management support, and lack of clear system objectives. Similar factors apply to projects in any field. Critical success factors in information system implementation were found to change with project stages, but to primarily influence the motivation of the project team as well as the three primary factors of user involvement, top management support, and clear system objectives.

Glossary

Cold turkey approach. System implementation by cutting the old system and plugging in the new at one moment.

Corresponding failure. Failure of a system to meet its design objectives.

Expectation failure. Failure of a project to meet its stakeholder's expectations.

Interaction failure. Condition of a system not being used by its intended users.

Parallel installation. Implementation of a system while maintaining the old system until assured that the new system functions appropriately.

Pilot operation approach. Implementation of a system on a small scale prior to cutting the old system.

Process failure. Failure of a project to meet time and budget requirements.

Quality control. Means taken to assure that designed product quality is present.

User training. Training provided to users to demonstrate what the system will do, and how the users can apply the new system.

PMBOK Items Relating to Chapter 8

Project success should be measured in terms of completing the project within the constraints of scope, time, cost, quality, resources, and risk as approved between the project managers and senior management.

Executing Process Group—those processes performed to completion as defined in the project management plan to satisfy project specifications.

4.3 Direct and Manage Project Work—the process of leading and performing the work defined in the project management plan and implementing approved changes to achieve the project's objectives.

4.7 Close Project or Phase—activity of finalizing project requirements.

6.6 Control Schedule—take actions to keep the project on schedule.

7.4 Control Costs—Audit accounting transactions related to the project.

Thought Questions

1. How could a project that performs according to technical specifications, and is completed on time and within budget, be considered a failure?

2. Describe a project champion.

Note

1. Boehm (1981).

References

Alkass, S., M. Mazerolle, and F. Harris. 1996. "Construction Delay Analysis Techniques." *Construction Management and Economics* 14, pp. 375–394.

Boehm, B.W. 1981. *Software Engineering Economics.* Englewood Cliffs, NJ: Prentice-Hall.

Conforto, E.C., F. Salum, D.C. Amaral, S. Luis da Silva, and L.F. Magnanini de Almeida. 2014. Can Agile Project Management Be Adopted by Industries Other Than Software Development? *Project Management Journal* 45, no. 3, pp. 21–34.

Kraiem, Z.M., and J.E. Diekmann. 1987. "Concurrent Delays in Construction Projects." *Journal of Construction Engineering Management* 113, no. 4, pp. 591–602.

Olson, D.L. 2004. *Introduction to Information Systems Project Management.* 2nd ed. Englewood Cliffs, NJ: McGraw-Hill/Irwin.

Sundararajan, S., M. Bhasi, and P.K. Vijayaraghavan. 2013. "Case Study on Risk Management Practice in Large Offshore-Outsourced Agile Software Projects." *IET Software* 8, no. 6, pp. 245–257.

Tanner, M., and A. Mackinnon. 2015. "Sources of Interruptions Experienced During a Scrum Sprint." *The Electronic Journal of Information Systems Evaluation* 18, no. 1, pp. 3–18.

Yordanova, S., and K. Toshkov. 2019. "An Agile Methodology for Managing Business Processes in an IT Company." *Biznes Upraivlenie*, no.3, pp. 72–90.

About the Author

David L. Olson is the James & H.K. Stuart Professor in MIS and Chancellor's Professor at the University of Nebraska. He has published his research in over 200 refereed journal articles, primarily on the topic of multiple objective decision making, information technology, supply chain risk management, and data mining. He teaches management science, business analytics, and supply chain management. He has authored over 30 books, to include *Decision Aids for Selection Problems*, and books on risk management, project management, and business analytics. He is associate editor of *Decision Support Systems; IEEE Transactions on Systems, Man, and Cybernetics*; and *Decision Sciences* and is coeditor in chief of *International Journal of Services Sciences*. He has made hundreds of presentations at international and national conferences on research topics. He is a member of the Decision Sciences Institute, the Institute for Operations Research and Management Sciences, and the Multiple Criteria Decision Making Society. He was a Lowry Mays endowed professor at Texas A&M University from 1999 to 2001. He had received the Raymond E. Miles Distinguished Scholar award for 2002 and was a James C. and Rhonda Seacrest Fellow from 2005 to 2006. He was awarded the Best Enterprise Information Systems Educator by IFIP in 2006. He is a fellow of the Decision Sciences Institute.

Index

OTHER TITLES IN OUR PORTFOLIO AND PROJECT MANAGEMENT COLLECTION

Timothy Kloppenborg, *Editor*

- *Project Management Essentials, Second Edition* by Kathryn N. Wells and Timothy J. Kloppenborg
- *Passion, Persistence, and Patience: Key Skills for Achieving Project Success* by Alfonso Bucero
- *Implementing Information Systems Projects: A Managerial Perspective* by D P Goyal
- *Adaptive Project Planning* by Christopher Worsley
- *Project Portfolio Management, Second Edition: A Model for Improved Decision Making* by Clive N. Enoch
- *The Lost Art of Planning Projects* by Louise Worsley and Christopher Worsley
- *Project Communication from Start to Finish: The Dynamics of Organizational Success* by Geraldine E. Hynes
- *Executing Global Projects: A Practical Guide to Applying the PMBOK Framework in the Global Environment* by James Marion and Tracey Richardson
- *Capital Project Management, Volume I: Capital Project Strategy* by Robert N. McGrath
- *Capital Project Management, Volume II: Capital Project Finance* by Robert N. McGrath
- *Capital Project Management, Volume III: Evolutionary Forces* by Robert N. McGrath
- *Projects, Programs, and Portfolios in Strategic Organizational Transformation* by James Jiang and Gary Klein
- *How to Fail at Change Management: A Manager's Guide to the Pitfalls of Managing Change* by James Marion and John Lewis

Announcing the Business Expert Press Digital Library

Concise e-books business students need for classroom and research

This book can also be purchased in an e-book collection by your library as

- *a one-time purchase,*
- *that is owned forever,*
- *allows for simultaneous readers,*
- *has no restrictions on printing, and*
- *can be downloaded as PDFs from within the library community.*

Our digital library collections are a great solution to beat the rising cost of textbooks. E-books can be loaded into their course management systems or onto students' e-book readers. The **Business Expert Press** digital libraries are very affordable, with no obligation to buy in future years. For more information, please visit **www.businessexpertpress.com/librarians**. To set up a trial in the United States, please email **sales@businessexpertpress.com**.